Country Living
COUNTRY MORNINGS
Cookbook

Country Living

COUNTRY MORNINGS
Cookbook

EDITED BY LUCY WING

HEARST BOOKS
New York

Printed in Singapore
First Edition
1 2 3 4 5 6 7 8 9 10

Country Living Staff
Rachel Newman, Editor
Lucy Wing, Contributing Food Editor
Joanne Lamb Hayes, Food Editor
Mary Clifford, Associate
Louise Fiore, Assistant

Produced by Smallwood and Stewart,
New York City

Designed by Sue Rose

Library of Congress Catalog Card Number: 88-083699
ISBN: 0-688-06639-9

Country Living

COUNTRY MORNINGS

Cookbook

Contents

Foreword

As we celebrate our first ten years of publication, we have undertaken the task of publishing our first cookbook.

Mornings are the purest time of day. And a hearty country breakfast, cooked up simply and served caringly, feeds both body and soul. Frankly, we are a bit puzzled by all the attention this most wonderful of meals has received during the last few years—we at Country Living have been touting it since our earliest issues. Our pages are full of recipes for biscuits, muffins, coffeecakes, breads, griddle cakes, and waffles. We have long praised the joys of putting up your own preserves when the fruits are in season, as well as the pure pleasure of eating summer's fruits and berries when they are bursting with sun-ripened flavor. At Country Living, freshly gathered eggs, creamy grits, and smoky slabs of bacon are prepared as lovingly—and as carefully—as the fanciest of party dishes.

Our readers have responded enthusiastically, some writing to tell us of their family's enjoyment of a good country breakfast, others to share favorite recipes and traditions passed to them from earlier generations. It is in this spirit of tradition and sharing, then, that we have prepared the Country Living Country Mornings Cookbook. Here are our most popular breakfast recipes, generously seasoned with a good measure of breakfast folklore and gently mixed together. Now we're proud to offer them to you, with the hope that from our family to your family, a new tradition will take root.

In preparing this book, we have relied on the contributions of past food editors Freddi Greenberg, Amy Chatham Scotton, and Lucy Wing, with our present food editor Joanne Lamb Hayes. Lucy Wing, now a contributing editor, has coordinated the production of this book.

RACHEL NEWMAN, *Editor, Country Living*

Introduction

Breakfast in the country is an important meal. Farmers who rise with the sun depend on a full meal of eggs, meat, toast, and fresh fruit—they need a good share of protein and energy after early morning chores. Folks who migrate to the country on weekends look forward to leisurely meals at well-spread tables where the conversation is relaxed, the newspaper very much in evidence, and the coffee plentiful and hot. . .

So many early morning recipes—created out of pure American ingenuity—are part of today's country traditions. Many of our favorites were born of a necessity to "make do" with whatever was available. The early settlers learned how to use every last bit of food; scrapple, for example, is the legacy of thrifty Pennsylvania Dutch farmwives who made it from discarded parts of the butchered hog. And soul food, found so often on Southern breakfast tables in the form of grits, corn fritters, and ham with redeye gravy, was devised by slaves who adapted their native African cooking style to the meager ends they were offered on the plantation. Sourdough breads, rolls, and pancakes are a gift of homesteading pioneers who carried "starters" of natural yeast to leaven their bread.

When we think of the best of country cooking, we think of food that is taken right from the land, from right outside our kitchen door. In our cookbook, we've included recipes that rely on America's native fruits and vegetables. Pumpkins, which are sometimes called American squash, are here in Spicy Pumpkin Muffins and Cinnamon Pumpkin Pancakes. Black walnuts are distinctly American, and we've combined them with an indigenous fruit, the cranberry. Our Black Walnut Cranberry Bread may well become a tradition on your breakfast table. Our cookbook has recipes for Cranberry and Almond Muffins, Cranberries in Syrup, for Cranberry Braid and Cran-

berry Butter. Maple sugar and maple syrup are more delights introduced to us by the Indians. When we bake with the syrup, as in our Rich Maple Nut Bread, the unmistakably American flavor comes through. And when we convert that phrase "As American as apple pie" to the breakfast table, we get apples in all sorts of delicious varieties—paired with sausage or baked into rich butter, apples fried and apples frittered, to name a few.

Across America, the country table is a relaxed, friendly place. What is prepared for breakfast may vary from region to region, but the congenial atmosphere of the meal stays the same. New England kitchens, warmed by wood stoves, see their share of pancakes blanketed with pure maple syrup. Down South, the table might be on a wide veranda and the morning fare consist of salty country ham and light-as-air biscuits. Farther west, where the mountain air is thin and clear, eggs-over-easy, hash browns, flapjacks, and pots of strong coffee get the day off to a good start. In the Southwest, they like their food spicy, and so the salsa on the table is for spooning over the eggs, and jalapeño peppers are mixed into the batter for corn muffins. Californians put platters heaped with fresh fruit on the table, along with slabs of thick, dense wheat bread, and bowls of cool yogurt. Wherever you wander across America, you will find breakfast a welcoming, warm meal.

LUCY WING, *Editor,*
Country Mornings Cookbook

Some Notes on Techniques and Ingredients

When we use 'homemade' to describe the wholesome, freshly made foods that were served up by Mother or Grandmother, that is high praise in itself. And so it is for our families, who savor the goodness of the kitchen's bounty today. For us, much of the tedious labor of cooking and baking has been eliminated by technology, though the principles of home cooking are un-changed—the best-quality ingredients are carefully prepared and combined. . .

Whether it is sophisticated haute cuisine or our more relaxed country fare, the first rule of good cooking is to read the entire recipe before you begin. If it calls for lots of ingredients and steps, you may want to read it a second time.

Prepare whatever work surfaces you'll need, then assemble and "prep" the ingredients: measure flours and spices, grate or shred cheese, rinse and trim fruit and vegetables, separate eggs, and so on. Inspect the utensils you'll use to see that mixing bowls are not chipped, that electric mixer beaters are in good order, and that pots and spoons are impeccably grease- and dust-free. If baking pans are to be greased or lined, it's easier to do so before starting.

In the recipes that follow, you needn't sift flour unless specifically called for (light fluffing with a fork will nicely separate heavily packed flour). In our biscuits, muffins, and quick breads, baking powder is the double-acting type. Butter is lightly salted unless noted and to be sure of buying the freshest butter in the market, check the shelf date stamped on the carton or wrapper. We use commercial sour cream and buttermilk and large eggs. Try not to make substitutions unless they are suggested: chances are that using honey for sugar or whipped butter in place of stick will yield a disappointing dish.

Yeast, whether fresh, active dry, or rapid-rising, is temperamental. As yeast-risen breads and pastries usually involve more work and time than those leavened with baking powder or soda, it pays to take extra care to give yeast the atmospheric conditions it needs. The warm water or other liquid in which yeast is dissolved must be between 105° and 115°F, and when a recipe asks that a liquid be "warm," that should be no more than 115°F. Similarly, most yeast doughs require at least one rising, in a warm place, away from drafts. For Croissants and one or two other recipes, the dough should rise at room temperature, that is, between 70° and 75°F.

In Grandmother's kitchen, ingredients were measured in coffee cups and kitchen spoons or described in terms such as a "lump of butter the size of a walnut." Now, to achieve absolute accuracy, we measure ingredients with standard liquid and dry measuring cups and spoons. Use the specific pot or pan sizes we indicate; if a pan is too small, food may bubble over. Place a reliable thermometer in your oven and allow adequate time for preheating. When a recipe says "cool," it means bring the food to room temperature; "chill" means refrigerate. Bear in mind that recipe yields in servings are average-size portions; one person may comfortably eat two servings, and one teenager may comfortably eat much more than that.

The baking time we give will be accurate for most ovens, and we suggest that you not open the oven door until the shorter time has elapsed. For example, if the baking time is 25 to 35 minutes, open the door only after 25 minutes. Another way to test doneness is to insert a cake tester or toothpick into the center of the muffin, quick bread, or whatever; if it's clean when it is removed, the food is done.

Measuring Equivalents

1 tablespoon = 3 teaspoons

½ tablespoon = 1½ teaspoons

⅓ tablespoon = 1 teaspoon

1 cup = 16 tablespoons

½ cup = 8 tablespoons

½ cup = 4 ounces liquid

2 tablespoons = 1 ounce liquid

⅓ cup = 5 tablespoons plus 1 teaspoon

4 cups = 1 quart

2 cups = 1 pint

1 cup = ½ pint

4 quarts = 1 gallon

16 cups = 1 gallon

2 quarts = ½ gallon

8 cups = ½ gallon

1 pound = 16 ounces

1 ounce = 28.35 grams

1 gram = .035 ounces

Biscuits & Scones

The screen door slams, magnolia leaves cast dappled shadows on the lawn, and a mockingbird beckons. From the kitchen at the back of the house comes the familiar smell of frying ham mingling with the more subtle one of baking biscuits. A Southern breakfast is nearly ready.

Biscuits are a tradition in Southern households and have been since the last century when the technology was perfected for milling fine, smooth white flour. Until then, no one expected the grain carried to the local mill to come back in any form other than coarse-grained whole-wheat flour. This was baked into an acceptable loaf, but it did not compare with the delicate biscuits and breads that issued forth from large brick ovens once white flour was introduced.

Ironic as it may seem, the poorer folks had little access to this wondrous white flour. But, as the cooks for the wealthier families, they were the people who experimented with it. A cook who earned a reputation for turning out light, airy biscuits was treasured indeed. Recipes and methods were passed from generation to generation and today we quickly associate tender biscuits with rural Southern cooking.

Flaky, white biscuits are easy to make. One of the fastest of baked goods to put together, biscuits are also among the most reliable. People who make them with regularity barely have to measure the ingredients—a quick stir, a pat or two, and a fast roll-out are all it takes before the biscuits are popped in the oven. The dough should be handled only a little, but it does need the few seconds of kneading called for. The biscuits may be stamped out with a cutter or an upturned glass, but whichever you use, don't twist it in the dough. Scraps should be patted together and flattened, not rerolled; the dough will toughen. Although best if timed so that they are taken from the oven just as everyone is sitting down at the table, biscuits can be made ahead and frozen unbaked. Add five minutes to the baking time.

Scones resemble biscuits, and indeed might be considered their British cousins. They are commonplace on the tea table but being inherently rebellious, we Yanks find them inviting on the breakfast table as well. Scones, like biscuits, are simple to put together. They are generally heavier than biscuits, and often are studded with dried fruit and ginger, or made from nutritious oats. A hot scone eaten as the British do, with a dollop of crème fraîche or Devonshire cream and some chunky raspberry preserves, is a taste treat not to be missed on either side of the Atlantic.

Country Cheese Biscuits

A good sharp Cheddar, coarsely shredded and worked into a basic biscuit dough, turns a familiar breakfast bread into a hearty, flavorful one that will happily round out a morning meal of ham and eggs. Try to use only real Cheddar; processed cheeses don't have the same firm texture and true taste.

MAKES 2 DOZEN BISCUITS

> 2 cups all-purpose flour
> 2 teaspoons baking powder
> ⅛ teaspoon salt
> ½ cup (1 stick) butter or margarine
> 1 cup coarsely shredded Cheddar cheese
> ⅔ cup milk

1. Heat the oven to 450°F. Lightly grease 2 baking sheets. In a large bowl, combine the flour, baking powder, and salt. With a pastry blender or 2 knives, cut in the butter until the mixture resembles coarse crumbs.

2. Add the cheese and milk to the flour mixture; mix lightly with a fork until the mixture clings together and forms a ball of soft dough. Turn the dough onto a lightly floured surface and knead gently, turning 5 or 6 times.

3. With a floured rolling pin, roll the dough to ½-inch thickness. With a floured 2-inch cutter, cut the dough into rounds. Place the biscuits, 1 inch apart, on the greased baking sheet. Pat the dough scraps together, reroll, and cut out more biscuits. With a fork, pierce each biscuit several times.

4. Bake the biscuits 12 to 15 minutes, or until they are light brown.

Angel Biscuits

Sometimes called bride's biscuits, these extra-light biscuits reach celestial heights because they are leavened with both yeast and baking powder.

MAKES ABOUT 1 DOZEN BISCUITS

> 1 package active dry yeast
> ¼ cup warm water (105° to 115°F)
> 2 tablespoons sugar
> 3 cups all-purpose flour
> 1 tablespoon baking powder
> ½ teaspoon salt
> ½ cup (1 stick) butter or margarine
> ¾ cup milk

1. In a small bowl, sprinkle the yeast over the water. Stir in the sugar and set aside until the mixture is foamy, about 10 minutes.

2. In a medium-size bowl, combine the flour, baking powder, and salt. With a pastry blender or 2 knives, cut in the butter until the mixture resembles coarse crumbs. Add the yeast mixture and the milk; mix lightly with a fork until they are well combined.

3. Cover the dough with a clean cloth and let it rise in a warm place, away from drafts, until it is double in size, about 30 minutes.

4. Grease a large baking sheet. On a lightly floured surface, with a floured rolling pin, roll the dough to a ½-inch thickness. With a floured 3-inch cutter, cut the dough into rounds. Place the biscuits, 1 inch apart, on the baking sheet. Prick the tops with a fork. Pat the scraps together, reroll, and cut out more biscuits. Cover the dough with a clean cloth and let it rise again until it is double in size, about 45 minutes. Heat the oven to 375°F.

5. Bake the biscuits 15 to 18 minutes, or until they are golden and firm on top. Serve warm.

Good Plain Biscuits

(Photograph, page 21)

The very heart of the country kitchen, plain everyday biscuits combine basic ingredients with quick baking. Make them as close to breakfast as you can—they're best still warm from the oven.

MAKES 12 TO 14 BISCUITS

> 2 cups all-purpose flour
> 1 tablespoon baking powder
> ½ teaspoon salt
> 6 tablespoons butter or vegetable shortening
> ⅔ cup milk

1. Heat the oven to 450°F. In a large bowl, combine the flour, baking powder, and salt. With a pastry blender or 2 knives, cut in the butter until the mixture resembles coarse crumbs.

2. Add the milk to the flour mixture; mix lightly with a fork until the mixture clings together and forms a ball of soft dough. Turn the dough onto lightly floured surface and knead gently, turning 5 or 6 times.

3. With a floured rolling pin, roll the dough to ½-inch thickness. With a floured 2-inch cutter, cut the dough into rounds. Place the biscuits, 1 inch apart, on an ungreased baking sheet. Pat the dough scraps together, reroll, and cut out more biscuits.

4. Bake the biscuits 10 to 12 minutes, or until they are light brown.

Buttermilk Biscuits

Prepare as above but use 2 teaspoons baking powder and ¼ teaspoon baking soda in place of 1 tablespoon of baking powder. Add ¾ cup buttermilk in place of ⅔ cup milk.

Skillet Buttermilk Biscuits

In the days when every farmwife made butter, there was plenty of buttermilk in the larder. Thrifty cooks used it in all manner of baked goods, including biscuits. As the population moved west, the early settlers often had buttermilk too—but not always an oven. These biscuits are designed to be baked over an open fire, which, if the mood strikes, you may choose to do. However, we have modified the recipe for more conventional stovetop frying.

MAKES ABOUT 2½ DOZEN BISCUITS

> 3 to 4 cups vegetable oil or shortening
> 1 cup whole-wheat flour
> 1 cup all-purpose flour
> 1½ teaspoons baking soda
> ¼ teaspoon salt
> ¼ cup lard or vegetable shortening
> ¾ cup buttermilk

1. In a medium-size skillet, heat 1 inch of oil or enough shortening to make 1 inch to 370°F on a deep-fat thermometer.

2. While the oil is heating, in a large bowl, combine the flours, baking soda, and salt. With a pastry blender or 2 knives, cut in the lard until the mixture resembles coarse crumbs.

3. Add the buttermilk to the flour mixture; mix lightly with a fork until the mixture clings together and forms a ball of soft dough.

4. Break off pieces of dough and roll them into 1-inch balls. Flatten the balls and fry them until golden on each side, about 3 to 4 minutes in all. Drain the biscuits on paper towels or brown paper. Serve warm.

Sweet Potato Pecan Biscuits

(Photograph, page 23)

Sweet potato biscuits are as Southern as Scarlett O'Hara, and when flavored with pecans, become worthy of the best kitchens in Dixie. Also popular in the South, the self-rising flour we've used here has 1½ teaspoons baking powder and ½ teaspoon salt added to each cup of all-purpose flour.

MAKES 1½ DOZEN BISCUITS

¾ cup cold, mashed, cooked sweet potatoes
½ cup (1 stick) butter or margarine, melted and cooled
2 tablespoons brown sugar
½ cup milk
2 cups self-rising all-purpose flour
½ cup chopped pecans
1 tablespoon all-purpose flour

1. Heat the oven to 400°F. Lightly grease a baking sheet.

2. In a large bowl, combine the sweet potatoes, butter, and brown sugar. Stir in the milk and blend until smooth. Add the self-rising flour and stir until moistened. Dust the pecans with 1 tablespoon all-purpose flour and add to the dough.

3. Turn the dough onto a lightly floured surface and knead gently, turning 5 or 6 times. With a floured rolling pin, roll the dough to ½-inch thickness. With a floured 2-inch cutter, cut the dough into rounds. Place biscuits, 1 inch apart, on the greased baking sheet. Pat the dough scraps together, reroll, and cut out more biscuits.

4. Bake the biscuits 15 to 18 minutes, or until they are light brown.

Beaten Biscuits

These hard biscuits, described as being somewhere between biscuits and hockey pucks in texture, are real Southern cooking. And they defy anything you were ever told about the gentle treatment of pastry: Old recipes call for beating the dough with a mallet or the back of an ax for 20 or 30 minutes. These days, a food processor makes the job easier.

MAKES ABOUT 1½ DOZEN BISCUITS

3 cups all-purpose flour
1 teaspoon sugar
½ teaspoon salt
½ teaspoon baking powder
⅓ cup vegetable shortening or lard
¼ cup ice water
¼ cup milk

1. Heat the oven to 350°F. Lightly grease a large baking sheet. In a food processor, with the chopping blade, combine the flour, sugar, salt, and baking powder. Add the shortening and process just until the mixture resembles coarse crumbs.

2. Add the water and milk, a little at a time, until the dough balls up. Continue to process the dough until it is smooth, elastic, and slightly blistered.

3. On a floured surface, with a floured rolling pin, roll the dough to ½-inch thickness. With a floured 2-inch cutter, cut dough into rounds. Place the biscuits, 1 inch apart, on the greased baking sheet. Pat the dough scraps together, reroll, and cut out more biscuits. With a fork, pierce each biscuit twice in a parallel row.

4. Bake the biscuits 30 to 35 minutes, or until they start to brown on top and are golden brown on the bottom.

Country Ham with Redeye Gravy, page 106

Fried Apple Rings, page 167

Good Plain Biscuits, page 19

Breakfast Grits, page 116

Sweet Potato Pecan Biscuits, page 20

Black Walnut Cranberry Bread, page 44

23

Banana-Walnut Muffins, page 37

New England Cornmeal Biscuits

Early New England settlers quickly learned to use ground corn in place of far scarcer wheat flour. Here we combine white cornmeal with all-purpose flour to produce richly textured, flavorful biscuits, reminiscent of the hoe cakes and jonnycakes of earlier times.

MAKES 8 LARGE BISCUITS

> 1½ cups all-purpose flour
> ½ cup white cornmeal
> 1 tablespoon baking powder
> 1 tablespoon sugar
> ¼ teaspoon salt
> ¼ cup vegetable shortening
> ¼ cup water
> ¼ cup milk

1. Heat the oven to 450°F. Lightly grease a baking sheet. In a large bowl, combine the flour, cornmeal, baking powder, sugar, and salt. With a pastry blender or 2 knives, cut in the shortening until the mixture resembles coarse crumbs.

2. Add the water and milk to the flour mixture; mix lightly with a fork until the mixture clings together and forms a ball of soft dough. Turn the dough onto a lightly floured surface and knead gently, turning 5 or 6 times.

3. With a floured rolling pin, roll the dough to ½-inch thickness. With a floured 3-inch cutter, cut the dough into rounds. Place the biscuits, 1 inch apart, on the greased baking sheet. Pat the dough scraps together, reroll, and cut out more biscuits. With a fork, pierce each biscuit several times.

4. Bake the biscuits 12 to 15 minutes, or until they are light brown.

Rye Biscuits

Today, tangy rye flour is available in supermarkets as well as natural food stores, but it is not a flour we often bake with. Yet, when family farms were commonplace throughout rocky New England, the flour was a staple simply because rye flourishes in poor soil. It is not surprising, then, that rye flour turns up in any number of old recipes for baked goods.

MAKES 1 DOZEN LARGE BISCUITS

> 2 cups rye flour
> 2 cups all-purpose flour
> 4 teaspoons baking powder
> 4 teaspoons sugar
> 1 teaspoon salt
> ½ cup (1 stick) butter or margarine
> 1⅓ cups milk

1. Heat the oven to 450°F. Lightly grease a baking sheet. In a large bowl, combine the flours, baking powder, sugar, and salt. With a pastry blender or 2 knives, cut in the butter until the mixture resembles coarse crumbs.

2. Add the milk to the flour mixture; mix lightly with a fork until the mixture clings together and forms a ball of soft dough. Turn the dough onto a lightly floured surface and knead gently, turning 5 or 6 times.

3. With a floured rolling pin, roll the dough to ½-inch thickness. With a floured 3-inch cutter, cut the dough into rounds. Place the biscuits, 1 inch apart, on the greased baking sheet. Pat the dough scraps together, reroll, and cut out more biscuits. With a fork, pierce each several times.

4. Bake the biscuits 12 to 15 minutes, or until they are light brown.

Edinburgh Tea Room Scones

A recipe from the kitchen of a tea room in Scotland's capital city is the inspiration for our version of Edinburgh tea room scones. These are lovely with sweet, unsalted butter and Old English Lemon Curd (page 171), and of course, freshly brewed tea.

MAKES ABOUT 1½ DOZEN SCONES

> 2 cups all-purpose flour
> 2 teaspoons baking powder
> ½ teaspoon salt
> ¼ teaspoon baking soda
> 6 tablespoons butter or margarine
> ½ cup golden or dark seedless raisins
> ½ cup buttermilk
> 1 large egg
> 1 tablespoon milk
> 1 tablespoon sugar

1. Heat the oven to 425°F. Lightly grease a large baking sheet. In a large bowl, combine the flour, baking powder, salt, and baking soda. With a pastry blender or 2 knives, cut in the butter until the mixture resembles coarse crumbs. Mix in the raisins with a fork.

2. In a cup, beat together the buttermilk and egg, then add them to the flour mixture. Mix lightly with a fork until the mixture clings together and forms a ball of soft dough. Turn the dough onto a lightly floured surface and knead gently, turning 5 or 6 times.

3. With a floured rolling pin, roll the dough to ½-inch thickness. With a floured 2-inch biscuit cutter, cut dough into rounds. Place the scones, 1 inch apart, on the greased baking sheet. Pat the dough scraps together, reroll, and cut out more scones. Lightly brush the tops of the scones with milk and sprinkle with sugar.

4. Bake the scones 10 to 12 minutes, or until they are golden brown.

Ginger Scones

Crystals of preserved ginger bring a distinctive flavor and aroma to these sturdy scones. Serve them with a choice of your homemade preserves: Golden Orange Marmalade (page 172) and Lemony Pear Preserves (page 173).

MAKES 8 LARGE SCONES

> 4 cups all-purpose flour
> ¼ cup sugar
> 2 tablespoons baking powder
> 1 teaspoon salt
> 1 teaspoon ground ginger
> 1 cup (2 sticks) butter or margarine
> ½ cup coarsely chopped preserved ginger
> ½ cup dried currants
> 1 cup milk
> ⅓ cup syrup drained from preserved ginger

1. Heat the oven to 400°F. Lightly grease a large baking sheet. In a large bowl, combine the flour, sugar, baking powder, salt, and ground ginger. With a pastry blender or 2 knives, cut in the butter until the mixture resembles coarse crumbs.

2. Stir the chopped ginger and currants into the flour mixture. Add the milk and ginger syrup; mix lightly with a fork until the mixture clings together and forms a ball of soft dough. Turn the dough onto a lightly floured surface and knead gently, turning 5 or 6 times.

3. With a floured rolling pin, roll the dough to an 8-inch square. Cut the dough into four 4-inch squares. Cut each square diagonally to make 8 triangles in all. Place the scones, 1 inch apart, on the greased baking sheet.

4. Bake the scones 15 to 18 minutes, or until they are golden brown and firm.

Biscuits

If you run out of baking powder, try substituting ¼ teaspoon baking soda, ½ teaspoon cream of tartar, and ¼ teaspoon cornstarch for a teaspoon of baking powder.

Quick Currant Scones

British tradition dictates that scones be served with afternoon tea, along with rich clotted cream and homemade strawberry jam. We think these easy-to-make, substantial scones are simply splendid in the morning, too, with a steaming cup of coffee.

MAKES 1½ DOZEN SCONES

> 2½ cups buttermilk baking mix
> 2 tablespoons sugar
> ⅓ cup butter or margarine
> ½ cup dried currants
> ⅓ cup milk
> 2 large eggs
> 1 tablespoon milk
> 1 tablespoon sugar

1. Heat the oven to 450°F. Lightly grease a large baking sheet. In a large bowl, combine the baking mix and sugar. With a pastry blender or 2 knives, cut in the butter until the mixture resembles coarse crumbs. With a fork, mix in the currants.

2. In a cup, beat together the milk and eggs, then add them to the flour mixture. Mix lightly with a fork until the mixture clings together and forms a ball of soft dough. Turn the dough onto a lightly floured surface and knead gently, turning 5 or 6 times.

3. With a floured rolling pin, roll the dough to a 9-inch square. Cut this into nine 3-inch squares; cut each square diagonally into 2 triangles, for a total of 18 triangles. Place the scones, 1 inch apart, on the greased baking sheet. Lightly brush the tops of the scones with milk and sprinkle with sugar.

4. Bake the scones 12 to 15 minutes, or until they are golden brown.

Muffins & Quick Breads

Line a basket or a pretty dish with a gingham napkin and fill it with muffins—hot, tender, and a little sweet. Breakfast is a delicious meal . . . and muffins are one of the best things about it.

Hearty and robust or delicate and cake-like, all muffins have a place on the morning table. Chunky jams and preserves go well with full-flavored muffins, while the more subtle ones need only sweet butter, a little crème fraîche, or perhaps a spoonful of jelly. Some muffins, such as those filled with berries, need no accompaniment at all.

If you like high, rounded muffins, disregard all the instructions you have ever read which advise you to fill the muffin cups one-half or two-thirds full. Instead, fill the cups to the brim—especially if the batter is heavy or made with whole-wheat flour.

Standard in most kitchens is the 12-cup, 2½-inch diameter muffin-cupcake pan, and most of our recipes are designed for it. If your family loves muffins, buy a jumbo muffin pan or 6-ounce custard cups. In either, you can bake six or seven giant muffins with the batter for 12 regular-size ones. These tasty monsters need to bake about 10 minutes longer. Miniature muffins, or "gem" as they are called in some regions, are 1⅝-inches in diameter and will bake more quickly.

Muffins are so easy to make—the batter takes minutes to whip up and they bake quickly. Even if your family is small, make a full recipe and freeze any that are not eaten right away. In the time it takes to brew fresh coffee and bring in the morning paper, the frozen muffins can be reheated and ready to be set on the breakfast table. To freeze them, wrap completely cooled muffins in aluminum foil and enclose them in a plastic freezer bag. When you reheat them, leave them in the foil and put them in a preheated 350°F oven for 10 or 15 minutes until they are soft, moist, and hot. Unwrap them and bake them until they are crusty, or split them horizontally and toast them.

Quick breads are made from the same type of batter as muffins. They share the same uneven, sometimes cake-like crumb. They are the breads we fill with nuts and cranberries at Christmas, pumpkin puree near Thanksgiving, and zucchini at summer's end when the garden is overrun with the squash.

Most of these quick breads call for standard 9- by 5-inch loaf pans. In some recipes, though, the bread is made in a slightly smaller pan, one that measures 8½- by 4½-inches. For real country bread baking, cracklin' bread and Irish soda bread are baked in 9-inch cast-iron skillets. And with typical New England thrift, steamed brown bread is baked in old coffee cans. Quick breads very often benefit from being made a day ahead and wrapped tightly in foil to mellow their flavors.

Great Plains Wheat Muffins

Full of the goodness of wheat, these wholesome, hearty muffins taste wonderful on their own, yet are made even better by stirring a handful of chopped dried fruit or unsalted nuts into the batter.

MAKES 1 DOZEN MUFFINS

> 1 cup whole-wheat flour
> ¾ cup all-purpose flour
> ¼ cup unprocesed bran
> 4 teaspoons baking powder
> ½ teaspoon salt
> ⅓ cup butter or margarine
> 1 cup milk
> 1 large egg

1. Heat the oven to 400°F. Generously grease 12 muffin cups. In a large bowl, with a fork, combine the flours, bran, baking powder, and salt.

2. In a 1-quart saucepan, melt the butter. Cool it slightly. Stir in the milk, then beat in the egg. Stir the liquid into the flour mixture just until moistened; the batter will be lumpy. Divide the batter among the greased cups.

3. Bake the muffins 20 to 25 minutes, or until a cake tester comes out clean. Remove the muffins from the cups and serve warm.

Carrot-Raisin Muffins

Flecked with shredded carrots and studded with plenty of plump raisins, these nutritious muffins need no butter or spread. Make a batch for those weekday mornings when you need breakfast in a hurry but don't want to skimp on good taste or good health.

MAKES 1 DOZEN MUFFINS

> 1 cup all-purpose flour
> 1 cup whole-wheat flour
> 2½ teaspoons baking powder
> 1 teaspoon ground cinnamon
> ½ teaspoon baking soda
> ½ teaspoon salt
> 1 cup coarsely shredded carrots
> ½ cup dark seedless raisins
> ¾ cup milk
> ¼ cup vegetable oil
> ¼ cup honey
> 1 large egg

1. Heat the oven to 400°F. Generously grease 12 muffin cups. In a large bowl, with a fork, combine the flours, baking powder, cinnamon, baking soda, and salt. Stir in the carrots and raisins.

2. In a 2-cup measuring cup or a small bowl, combine the milk, oil, honey, and egg. Stir the liquid into the flour mixture just until moistened; the batter will be lumpy. Divide the batter among the greased cups.

3. Bake the muffins 20 to 25 minutes, or until a cake tester comes out clean. Remove the muffins from the cups and serve warm.

Buttermilk Corn Muffins

Taste the creamy tang of buttermilk in these corn muffins, perfect with sturdy spreads such as Farmhouse Ginger Marmalade (page 174) or Old-Fashioned Peach Preserves (page 172).

MAKES 1 DOZEN REGULAR OR 2 DOZEN MINIATURE MUFFINS.

> 1½ cups yellow or white cornmeal
> ½ cup all-purpose flour
> 4 teaspoons baking powder
> 1 tablespoon sugar
> ½ teaspoon salt
> ¼ cup (½ stick) butter or margarine
> ¾ cup buttermilk
> 2 large eggs

1. Heat the oven to 425°F. Generously grease 12 regular or 24 miniature muffin cups. In a large bowl, with a fork, combine the cornmeal, flour, baking powder, sugar, and salt.

2. In a 1-quart saucepan, melt the butter. Cool it slightly. Stir in the buttermilk, then beat in the eggs. Stir the liquid into the flour mixture just until moistened; the batter will be lumpy. Divide the batter among the greased cups.

3. Bake the regular muffins 15 to 20 minutes, or the miniature ones 10 to 15 minutes. A cake tester should come out clean. Let them stand 5 minutes before removing them from the cups, and serve warm.

Raisin Bran Muffins

A quick look at the ingredients for our raisin bran muffins will tell you that they will be one of the most nutritious treats you can offer your family.

MAKES 1 DOZEN MUFFINS

> 1½ cups unprocessed bran
> 1¼ cups milk
> 1½ cups all-purpose flour
> ⅓ cup sugar
> 1 tablespoon baking powder
> 1 teaspoon ground cinnamon
> ½ teaspoon ground nutmeg
> ½ teaspoon salt
> ¼ teaspoon ground cloves
> ½ cup dark seedless raisins
> ½ cup (1 stick) butter or margarine
> ¼ cup molasses
> 1 large egg

1. In a medium-size bowl, combine the bran and the milk. Stir to moisten the bran and let stand 10 minutes.

2. Heat the oven to 400°F. Generously grease 12 muffin cups. In a large bowl, with a fork, combine the flour, sugar, baking powder, cinnamon, nutmeg, salt, and cloves. Stir in the raisins.

3. In a 1-quart saucepan, melt the butter. Cool it slightly. Stir in the molasses and the egg. Stir the butter mixture into the bran mixture until well mixed, then stir into the flour mixture just until moistened. The batter will be lumpy. Divide the batter among the greased cups.

4. Bake the muffins 15 to 20 minutes, or until a cake tester comes out clean. Remove the muffins from the cups and serve warm.

Blueberry-Cheese Muffins

Yes, this is an unusual combination, but blueberries and cheese are natural partners: The mild flavor of the Lorraine cheese plays up to the slightly sassy blueberries.

MAKES 1½ DOZEN MUFFINS

> 3 cups all-purpose flour
> 1 tablespoon baking powder
> ½ teaspoon baking soda
> ⅛ teaspoon salt
> ½ cup milk
> ½ cup sour cream
> ½ cup shredded Lorraine cheese
> 2 teaspoons vanilla extract
> ½ cup (1 stick) butter or margarine, softened
> 1 cup firmly packed light-brown sugar
> 2 large eggs
> 2 cups blueberries
> 1 tablespoon granulated sugar
> ½ teaspoon ground cinnamon

1. Heat the oven to 400°F. Line 18 muffin cups with fluted paper cups. On a sheet of waxed paper, sift together 2¾ cups flour, the baking powder, baking soda, and salt. In a small bowl, blend the milk, sour cream, cheese, and vanilla.

2. In a large bowl, with an electric mixer on high speed, beat the butter, brown sugar, and eggs until light and fluffy. On low speed, alternately add the flour mixture and the milk mixture to the butter mixture. Beat until well blended.

3. In a small bowl, combine the blueberries with the remaining ¼ cup flour. Carefully fold the blueberries into the batter. In a cup, mix together the granulated sugar and cinnamon. Divide the batter among the lined muffin cups. Sprinkle the tops of the muffins with some cinnamon-sugar.

4. Bake the muffins 18 to 20 minutes, or until a cake tester comes out clean. Remove the muffins from the cups and serve warm.

Poppy Seed-Sour Cream Muffins

Found in plentiful supply at almost any bakery, poppy seeds are a smart addition to your kitchen spice shelf. Of course they're wonderful on homemade rolls and breads, but try them with other foods. Sprinkle some over a platter of pale scrambled eggs or a mound of home fries, or bake a batch of our favorite poppy seed muffins. Delicately flavored and enriched with sour cream, these require only a bit of butter and a dollop of raspberry or peach jam.

MAKES 1 DOZEN MUFFINS

> 2 cups all-purpose flour
> ¼ cup poppy seeds
> ½ teaspoon salt
> ¼ teaspoon baking soda
> ½ cup (1 stick) butter or margarine, softened
> ¾ cup sugar
> 2 large eggs
> ¾ cup sour cream
> 1 teaspoon vanilla extract

1. Heat the oven to 400°F. Generously grease 12 muffin cups.

2. In a large bowl, combine the flour, poppy seeds, salt, and baking soda. In a medium-size bowl, with electric mixer on high speed, beat the butter and sugar until light and fluffy. Reduce the speed to medium and beat in the eggs, one at a time, until well blended. Beat in the sour cream and the vanilla.

3. With a rubber spatula, fold the butter mixture into the flour mixture just until moistened; the batter will be lumpy. Divide the batter among the greased cups.

4. Bake the muffins 15 to 20 minutes, or until a cake tester comes out clean. Remove the muffins from the cups and serve warm.

Zucchini Whole-wheat Muffins

A standard item in most every vegetable garden we've ever seen, zucchini is a crop as abundant as it is versatile. Shredded and mixed with whole-wheat flour, it creates a muffin that is especially healthful.

MAKES 10 MUFFINS

1½ cups coarsely shredded zucchini
1 cup all-purpose flour
1 cup whole-wheat flour
¼ cup sugar
4 teaspoons baking powder
1 teaspoon grated lemon rind
½ teaspoon salt
⅓ cup butter or margarine
1 cup milk
1 large egg

1. Heat the oven to 400°F. Generously grease ten 3-inch muffin cups. Place the shredded zucchini on a small piece of cheesecloth or in a strainer. Squeeze or press to remove as much moisture as possible. Set aside the zucchini to drain on paper towels.

2. In a large bowl, with a fork, combine the flours, sugar, baking powder, lemon rind, and salt. Fold in the zucchini.

3. In a 1-quart saucepan, melt the butter. Cool it slightly. Stir in the milk, then beat in the egg. Stir the liquid into the flour mixture just until moistened; the batter will be lumpy. Divide the batter among the greased cups.

4. Bake the muffins 20 to 25 minutes, or until a cake tester comes out clean. Let them stand 5 minutes before removing them from the cups and serve them warm.

Chocolate-Chip Pecan Muffins

We can thank the South for pecans. From Florida north to Delaware, and from Virginia west to Texas and Oklahoma, each fall brings the harvest of these delicious nuts. For breakfast, we enjoy them in luxurious muffins rich with chocolate chips.

MAKES 1 DOZEN MUFFINS

> 4 cups all-purpose flour
> 1 cup firmly packed light-brown
>   sugar
> 4 teaspoons baking powder
> ½ teaspoon salt
> 1 cup semisweet chocolate chips
> ½ cup chopped pecans
> ½ cup (1 stick) butter or margarine
> 1½ cups milk
> 2 large eggs
> 1 tablespoon vanilla extract
> 1 tablespoon granulated sugar

1. Heat the oven to 375°F. Generously grease and flour 12 muffin cups. In a large bowl, with a fork, combine the flour, brown sugar, baking powder, and salt. Stir in the chocolate chips and pecans.

2. In a 1-quart saucepan, melt the butter. Cool it slightly. With a wire whisk, stir in the milk, eggs, and vanilla. Stir the liquid into the flour mixture just until moistened; the batter will be lumpy. Divide the batter among the prepared cups. Sprinkle the tops of the muffins with granulated sugar.

3. Bake the muffins 15 to 20 minutes, -or until a cake tester comes out clean. Remove the muffins from the cups and serve warm.

Spring Rhubarb Muffins

For moist, fresh-tasting muffins, combine the tartness of rhubarb, the tang of buttermilk, and a good measure of brown sugar. Fresh rhubarb is available only in the early spring, so do make these while you can. Be sure to discard the leaves, which are poisonous.

MAKES 1½ DOZEN MUFFINS

> ¾ pound rhubarb without tops
> 2½ cups all-purpose flour
> 1 teaspoon baking powder
> 1 teaspoon baking soda
> ½ teaspoon salt
> ¼ teaspoon ground nutmeg
> ½ cup chopped walnuts or pecans
> 1¼ cups buttermilk
> 1 cup firmly packed light-brown sugar
> ½ cup vegetable oil
> 1 large egg
> 2 teaspoons vanilla extract

1. Heat the oven to 375°F. Generously grease 18 muffin cups. Trim the ends and any remaining leaves from the rhubarb. Rinse the stalks carefully and dry with paper towels. Coarsely chop the rhubarb.

2. In a large bowl, with a fork, combine the flour, baking powder, baking soda, salt, and nutmeg. Stir in the nuts. Fold in the chopped rhubarb.

3. In a small bowl, combine the buttermilk, brown sugar, oil, egg, and vanilla. Stir the liquid into the flour mixture just until moistened; the batter will be lumpy. Divide the batter among the greased cups.

4. Bake the muffins 18 to 20 minutes, or until a cake tester comes out clean. Let them stand 5 minutes before removing them from the cups and serve them warm.

Wenatchee Applesauce Muffins

Wenatchee, Washington is the apple-growing center of the Northwest. More than thirty percent of the nation's apples are grown in this area and, as a result, apple recipes are almost as abundant as the fruit itself.

MAKES 1 DOZEN MUFFINS

2 cups all-purpose flour
½ cup firmly packed light-brown
    sugar
1 tablespoon baking powder
½ teaspoon baking soda
½ teaspoon salt
½ teaspoon ground cinnamon
½ teaspoon ground nutmeg
½ cup dark seedless raisins
¼ cup (½ stick) butter or margarine
1 cup thick applesauce
¼ cup milk
1 large egg

1. Heat the oven to 425°F. Generously grease 12 muffin cups. In a large bowl, with a fork, combine the flour, sugar, baking powder, baking soda, salt, cinnamon, and nutmeg. Stir in the raisins.

2. In a 1-quart saucepan, melt the butter. Cool it slightly. Stir in the applesauce, milk, and egg. Stir the liquid into the flour mixture just until moistened; the batter will be lumpy. Divide the batter among the greased cups.

3. Bake the muffins 15 to 20 minutes, or until a cake tester comes out clean. Let them stand 5 minutes before removing them from the cups and serve them warm.

Coffee Praline Muffins

How could you go wrong with muffins that marry two of the best flavors of New Orleans: coffee and sugared pecans? These are divine with a delicate cup of Café au Lait (page 187) and a slice of honeydew melon.

MAKES 10 MUFFINS

1¾ cups all-purpose flour
⅓ cup firmly packed light-brown
    sugar
1 tablespoon baking powder
¼ teaspoon salt
½ cup coarsely chopped pecans
½ cup (1 stick) butter or margarine
¾ cup milk
2 tablespoons instant coffee
1 teaspoon vanilla extract
1 large egg
1 tablespoon granulated sugar

1. Heat the oven to 375°F. Generously grease 10 muffin cups. In a large bowl, with a fork, combine the flour, brown sugar, baking powder, and salt. Set aside 2 tablespoons pecans; add the remaining pecans to the flour mixture.

2. In a 1-quart saucepan, melt the butter. Cool it slightly. With a wire whisk, stir in the milk, instant coffee, vanilla, and egg. Beat until the coffee is dissolved. Stir the liquid into the flour mixture just until moistened. Divide the batter among the greased cups. Sprinkle the tops of the muffins with some granulated sugar and the reserved pecans.

3. Bake the muffins 18 to 20 minutes, or until a cake tester comes out clean. Remove the muffins from the cups and serve warm.

Cranberry and Almond Muffins

(Photograph, page 117)

Before dawn on chilly fall mornings, farmers head for the cranberry bogs to start the day's harvest. Whether the berries are scooped up from flooded bogs or picked "dry," they are available fresh for only a brief time. Adding them to muffin batter is a good way to enjoy the zesty flavor of these native American berries.

MAKES 6 JUMBO OR 12 REGULAR MUFFINS

> 1¾ cups all-purpose flour
> ½ cup whole-wheat flour
> ¾ cup sugar
> 1 tablespoon baking powder
> ½ teaspoon baking soda
> ½ teaspoon salt
> ½ teaspoon ground nutmeg
> 1 cup cranberries, each cut in half
> ½ cup sliced natural almonds
> ⅓ cup butter or margarine
> 1 cup milk
> 1 large egg

1. Heat the oven to 375°F or 400°F for regular muffins. Generously grease six jumbo or 12 regular muffin cups. If you are using the custard cups, arrange them on a small jelly-roll pan for easier handling.

2. In a large bowl, with a fork, combine the flours, sugar, baking powder, baking soda, salt, and nutmeg. Add the cranberries and almonds. Toss to mix well and set aside.

3. In a 1-quart saucepan, melt the butter. Cool it slightly. Stir in the milk, then beat in the egg. Stir the liquid into the flour mixture just until moistened; the batter will be lumpy. Divide the batter among the greased cups.

4. Bake the jumbo muffins 30 to 35 minutes, or the regular ones 20 minutes. A cake tester should come out clean. Let the muffins stand 5 minutes before removing them from the cups. Serve warm.

Banana-Walnut Muffins

(Photograph, page 24)

As comforting as they are nutritious, bananas bring their characteristic flavor to any number of cakes, breads, and muffins; if Nature hadn't created them, a baker would surely have contrived the banana. Bolstered with wheat germ and walnuts, these muffins are most appealing on winter mornings, piled into a straw basket and passed with a thick wedge of sharp Cheddar.

MAKES 1 DOZEN MUFFINS

> 1½ cups all-purpose flour
> 1 cup wheat germ
> ½ cup firmly packed light-brown sugar
> 1 tablespoon baking powder
> 1 teaspoon salt
> 1 teaspoon ground nutmeg
> ½ cup chopped walnuts
> ¼ cup (½ stick) butter or margarine
> 1 cup mashed, ripe banana (2 large)
> ½ cup milk
> 2 large eggs

1.   Heat the oven to 425°F. Generously grease 12 muffin cups. In a large bowl, with a fork, combine the flour, wheat germ, sugar, baking powder, salt, and nutmeg. Stir in the nuts.

2.   In a 1-quart saucepan, melt the butter. Cool it slightly. Stir in the banana, milk, and eggs. Stir the liquid into the flour mixture just until moistened; the batter will be lumpy. Divide the batter among the cups.

3.   Bake the muffins 20 to 25 minutes, or until a cake tester comes out clean. Remove the muffins from the cups and serve warm.

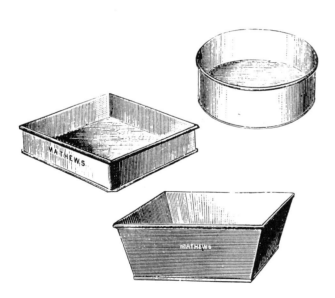

Spicy Pumpkin Muffins

For sheer versatility, consider the pumpkin. You can treat pumpkin as a vegetable: as a side dish for roasted meats, in a vegetable stew or chowder, or in pumpkin soup. Or you can use it as you would a fruit: in pie, ice cream, a dessert souffle, and in sweet breakfast muffins. If that is not enough, you can carve a great toothy grin on your pumpkin for a fantastic Halloween decoration.

MAKES 1 DOZEN MUFFINS

> 1½ cups all-purpose flour
> 6 tablespoons sugar
> 1 tablespoon baking powder
> ½ teaspoon salt
> ½ teaspoon ground cinnamon
> ½ teaspoon ground nutmeg
> ½ cup golden raisins
> ¼ cup (½ stick) butter or margarine
> 1 cup pumpkin puree (fresh or canned)
> ½ cup milk
> 1 large egg

1.   Heat the oven to 400°F. Generously grease 12 muffin cups. In a large bowl, with a fork, combine the flour, sugar, baking powder, salt, cinnamon, and nutmeg. Stir in the raisins.

2.   In a 1-quart saucepan, melt the butter. Cool it slightly. Stir in the pumpkin, milk, and egg. Stir the liquid into the flour mixture just until moistened; the batter will be lumpy. Divide the batter among the greased cups.

3.   Bake the muffins 15 to 20 minutes, or until a cake tester comes out clean. Remove the muffins from the cups and serve warm.

Rich Lemon Muffins

In earlier centuries, lemons were prized for their medicinal and cosmetic qualities. Today, home cooks rely on them in countless recipes for every meal of the day. At breakfast, our lemon muffins are doubly enriched with the juice and rind of the fresh fruit. When the season is right, serve these side by side with dainty little bowls of summer berries and sweet, heavy cream.

MAKES 1 DOZEN MUFFINS

> 2 cups all-purpose flour
> ½ cup plus 2 tablespoons sugar
> 1 tablespoon baking powder
> ½ teaspoon salt
> ½ cup (1 stick) butter or margarine
> Finely grated rind of 1 lemon
> ½ cup fresh lemon juice
> 2 large eggs

1. Heat the oven to 400°F. Generously grease 12 muffin cups. In a large bowl, with a fork, combine the flour, ½ cup sugar, baking powder, and salt.

2. In a 1-quart saucepan, melt the butter. Cool it slightly. Stir in the lemon rind and juice, then beat in the eggs. Stir the liquid into the flour mixture just until moistened; the batter will be lumpy. Divide the batter among the greased cups. Sprinkle the tops of the muffins with the remaining 2 tablespoons sugar.

3. Bake the muffins 15 to 20 minutes, or until a cake tester comes out clean. Remove the muffins from the cups and serve warm.

Savory Cheddar Muffins

Savory muffins are ideal for breakfasts of robust, hearty dishes. We recommend Cheddar muffins with Sausage with Apples and Herbs (page 110), Sonora Omelet (page 96), or your everyday bacon and eggs.

MAKES 1 DOZEN MUFFINS

> 1½ cups all-purpose flour
> ½ cup yellow or white cornmeal
> 1 tablespoon baking powder
> ½ teaspoon salt
> Pinch of ground red pepper
> ¼ cup (½ stick) butter or margarine
> 1 cup milk
> 1 large egg
> 1¼ cups coarsely shredded sharp
>   Cheddar cheese

1. Heat the oven to 425°F. Generously grease 12 muffin cups. In a large bowl, with a fork, combine the flour, cornmeal, baking powder, salt, and red pepper.

2. In a 1-quart saucepan, melt the butter. Cool it slightly. Stir in the milk, then beat in the egg. Stir the liquid into the flour mixture just until moistened; the batter will be lumpy. Stir 1 cup of the cheese into the batter. Divide the batter among the greased cups. Sprinkle about 1 teaspoon of the remaining cheese over each muffin.

3. Bake the muffins 15 to 20 minutes, or until a cake tester comes out clean. Remove the muffins from the cups and serve warm.

Morning Entertaining

No wonder brunch is such a popular meal in America: It's early in a new day, everyone is restored and refreshed, and the food is as relaxed and casual as a country cook can make it. Some yeast-based breads and coffeecakes do take a little more time, but most of our breakfast recipes are simply and quickly put together.

If successful entertaining looks effortless, this is even truer for brunch, when excess seems only to detract from the leisurely atmosphere. Prepare as much of the meal as possible in advance and spend a little extra time laying the table so that it is ready to welcome guests. Begin with a pretty cloth smoothed over the table and topped with a length of antique lace. Slip out to the garden to gather some fresh flowers to put in an old pewter pitcher or a glass milk bottle. Line the pastry or muffin basket with your prettiest napkin, or some paper doilies; set loaves of homemade bread on wood cutting boards. Scatter crocks packed with flavored butters and jars of your homemade luscious jams and preserves about the table for guests to choose from. To save space, pile fresh fruit on a pedestal-base cake or candy dish. Plates needn't match, just balance: use one of a kind or pairs of patterns. Do give everyone a big mug for coffee . . . plenty of fresh, hot coffee. Finally, open the curtains to let the sun stream in, then sit back, relax, and enjoy good food with good friends in your country home.

Golden-Raisin Honey Loaf

Amber honey, golden raisins, light brown sugar— all baked in a sweet loaf that's as good for breakfast as it is later with afternoon tea. While the bread bakes in less than an hour, it should sit overnight, well wrapped in foil, for its mellow flavors to blend.

MAKES 1 LOAF

2½ cups all-purpose flour
⅓ cup firmly packed light-brown sugar
2 teaspoons baking powder
1 teaspoon salt
½ teaspoon baking soda
½ cup vegetable shortening
1 cup golden raisins
2 large eggs
½ cup milk
½ cup honey
2 teaspoons grated lemon rind

1. Heat the oven to 325°F. Grease and flour a loaf pan. In a large bowl, combine the flour, brown sugar, baking powder, salt, and baking soda. With a pastry blender or 2 knives, cut in the shortening to resemble coarse crumbs. Stir in the raisins.

2. In a small bowl, beat the eggs, milk, honey, and lemon rind. Stir the honey mixture into the flour mixture just until the flour is moistened. Spoon the batter into the prepared pan.

3. Bake the loaf 50 minutes, or until a cake tester comes out clean. Cool the bread in the pan on a wire rack 10 minutes. Remove the bread from the pan and cool completely on the rack. Wrap the bread tightly in aluminum foil and let it stand overnight before slicing.

Chunky Zucchini Bread

Come late summer, every gardener, it seems, shares the same lament—what can we do with all that zucchini? Let the squash enter the breakfast arena by baking it into this easy quick bread, gently spiced with nutmeg and a hint of lemon.

MAKES 2 LOAVES

3 cups all-purpose flour
1½ cups sugar
4½ teaspoons baking powder
1 teaspoon salt
½ teaspoon ground nutmeg
1½ cups chopped zucchini
1½ cups chopped walnuts
1 cup vegetable oil
4 large eggs
2 teaspoons grated lemon rind

1. Heat the oven to 350°F. Grease and flour two 8½- by 4½-inch loaf pans. In a large bowl, combine the flour, sugar, baking powder, salt, and nutmeg. Stir in the zucchini and walnuts. In a small bowl, combine the oil, eggs, and lemon rind.

2. Stir the oil mixture into the flour mixture just until moistened. Spoon the batter into the prepared loaf pans.

3. Bake the loaves 1 hour, or until a cake tester comes out clean. Cool the breads in the pans on a wire rack 10 minutes. Remove the breads from the pans and cool completely on the rack. Wrap the breads tightly in aluminum foil and let them stand overnight before slicing.

Daily Bread, recipe page 50

French Bread, page 52

Lemon Poppy Seed Bread

Poppy seeds stirred into a basic batter give flavor and texture. Serve the bread at room temperature or toasted, with butter or, for a special treat, Honey Almond Butter (page 179).

MAKES 1 LOAF

> 3 cups all-purpose flour
> ½ cup poppy seeds (about 2¼ ounces)
> ¾ cup sugar
> 3½ teaspoons baking powder
> 1 teaspoon salt
> 2 large eggs
> 1½ cups milk
> ¼ cup vegetable oil
> Juice and finely grated rind of 1 lemon

1. Heat the oven to 350°F. Grease a loaf pan. In a large bowl, combine the flour, poppy seeds, sugar, baking powder, and salt. In a small bowl, beat the eggs; stir in the milk, oil, lemon juice and rind and add to the flour mixture.

2. Beat the batter 30 strokes, scraping down the side of the bowl often, until the batter is smooth. Spoon it into the greased pan. Bake 1 hour, or until a cake tester comes out clean.

3. Cool the bread in the pan on a wire rack 20 minutes. Remove the bread from the pan; cool it completely on the rack. Wrap the bread tightly in aluminum foil and let it stand overnight before slicing.

Banana Nut Bread

As the familiar sweet aroma fills the house, no one will be able to resist a slice of this dense, moist quick bread. Breakfast time? It's synonymous with banana bread and cream cheese.

MAKES 1 LOAF

> 1¾ cups all-purpose flour
> 1½ teaspoons baking powder
> ½ teaspoon baking soda
> ½ teaspoon ground cinnamon
> ¼ teaspoon salt
> ¼ cup (½ stick) butter or margarine
> ⅓ cup sugar
> 2 large eggs
> 1 cup mashed, ripe bananas (about 2 large)
> ¼ cup milk
> ½ cup chopped walnuts or pecans

1. Heat the oven to 350°F. Grease and flour a loaf pan. On a sheet of waxed paper, sift together the flour, baking powder, baking soda, cinnamon, and salt.

2. In a large bowl, with an electric mixer at medium-high speed, cream the butter and sugar until they are light and fluffy. Beat in the eggs, one at a time. On low speed, gradually add the dry ingredients and the bananas and milk, beating just until the batter is smooth. Fold in the nuts.

3. Spoon the batter into the prepared pan. Bake 55 to 60 minutes, or until it is golden on top and a cake tester comes out clean.

4. Cool the bread in the pan on a wire rack 5 minutes. Remove the bread from the pan and cool it completely on the rack. Wrap the bread tightly in aluminum foil and let it stand overnight before slicing.

Black Walnut Cranberry Bread

(Photograph, page 23)

Cranberries and black walnuts are both native to the Americas, are both in season in the autumn, and are both unmistakably tangy. They combine here in an old-fashioned quick bread, sure to provoke images of kitchen tables set with wide-mouthed milk bottles and crocks of churned butter. Black walnuts are one of the hardest nuts to crack—they come protected by a green, lime-size outer shell and an inside shell that holds the nutmeats in separate compartments. It's advisable to buy them already shelled from a reliable market or natural food store where you can be sure they have not grown stale.

MAKES 1 LOAF

> 2¾ cups all-purpose flour
> 1 cup sugar
> 1 tablespoon baking powder
> ½ teaspoon baking soda
> ½ teaspoon salt
> ¼ cup (½ stick) butter or margarine
> 2 teaspoons grated orange rind
> ½ cup fresh orange juice
> ½ cup milk
> 2 large eggs
> 1 cup fresh cranberries
> ½ cup black walnut pieces

1. Heat the oven to 350°F. Grease and flour a loaf pan. In a large bowl, combine the flour, sugar, baking powder, baking soda, and salt.

2. In a 1-quart saucepan, heat the butter just until melted. Remove from the heat. Stir in the orange rind, orange juice, and the milk. Beat in the eggs. Add the orange mixture to the flour mixture; stir just until moistened. Fold in the berries and nuts. Spoon the batter into the prepared pan.

3. Bake the loaf 60 to 70 minutes, or until a cake tester comes out clean. Cool the bread in the pan on a wire rack 10 minutes. Remove the bread from the pan and cool completely on the rack. Wrap the bread tightly in aluminum foil and let it stand overnight before slicing.

Rich Maple Nut Bread

Real maple syrup is terribly expensive; making the syrup from maple sap is time-consuming and laborious, a process that technology hasn't streamlined. But when you bake with it, you will be rewarded with its distinctive rich flavor, unmistakable in quick breads such as this one.

MAKES 1 LOAF

> 1 cup all-purpose flour
> ¾ cup whole-wheat flour
> 1 tablespoon baking powder
> 1 teaspoon salt
> ¼ teaspoon ground cinnamon
> ½ cup finely chopped walnuts
> ¼ cup (½ stick) butter or margarine
> ⅔ cup milk
> ⅓ cup maple syrup
> 1 large egg
> ½ teaspoon vanilla extract

TOPPING:
> 3 tablespoons finely chopped walnuts
> 2 tablespoons sugar
> ¼ teaspoon ground cinnamon

1. Heat the oven to 350°F. Grease a loaf pan. In a medium-size bowl, combine the flours, baking powder, salt, and cinnamon. Stir in the nuts.

2. In a 1-quart saucepan, melt the butter. Remove from the heat and stir in the milk and syrup. Beat in the egg and vanilla. Stir the milk mixture into the flour mixture until the mixture is just blended. Spoon the batter into the greased pan.

3. Prepare the Topping: In a cup, mix the walnuts, sugar, and cinnamon; sprinkle over batter. Bake 40 minutes, or until a cake tester comes out clean. Remove the bread from the pan and cool it completely on a wire rack. Wrap it tightly in aluminum foil and let it stand overnight before slicing.

Fruit Breads

When chopping dried fruit for quick breads or muffins, spray your knife with nonstick vegetable shortening spray so that the fruit won't stick.

Sour Cream Blueberry Banana Bread

A moist, berry-filled quick bread, this one is sweetened with ripe bananas as well as sugar. Try to bake it in high summer when the hillside blueberries are bursting with sweetness. You'll find that a generous slice is all you need for breakfast at the start of a lazy day in the country.

MAKES 1 LOAF

> 2 cups all-purpose flour
> 1 teaspoon baking soda
> ½ teaspoon salt
> ½ teaspoon ground cinnamon
> 1 cup (2 sticks) butter, softened
> ¾ cup sugar
> 2 large eggs
> 1 cup mashed, ripe bananas (2 large)
> ½ cup sour cream
> 1 cup blueberries
> ½ cup coarsely chopped pecans

1. Heat the oven to 350°F. Grease and flour a loaf pan. On a sheet of waxed paper, sift together the flour, baking soda, salt, and cinnamon.

2. In a large bowl, with an electric mixer on medium-high speed, cream the butter and sugar until they are light and fluffy. Add the eggs, bananas, and sour cream and beat until blended. Gradually beat in the flour mixture at low speed, and continue beating until the batter is smooth. Fold in the blueberries and the pecans.

3. Spoon the batter into the prepared pan. Bake 1 hour, or until the bread is golden on top and a cake tester comes out clean. Let the bread cool completely in the pan on a wire rack.

Irish Soda Bread

Baked in a cast-iron skillet, this simple farmhouse bread is a delicious example of the light, soda-raised breads of the luscious green countryside of Ireland. There, cooks have as many subtle variations for the homely loaf as there are chili variants in Texas. This version remains our favorite.

MAKES 1 LOAF

> 4½ cups all-purpose flour
> 3 tablespoons plus 1 teaspoon sugar
> 1 tablespoon caraway seeds
> 4 teaspoons baking powder
> ½ teaspoon baking soda
> 1 teaspoon salt
> 1 cup dried currants or dark seedless
>   raisins
> 2 cups buttermilk
> 1 teaspoon butter or margarine

1. Heat the oven to 350°F. Grease and flour a 9-inch cast-iron skillet. In a large bowl, mix 4 cups flour, 3 tablespoons sugar, caraway seeds, baking powder and soda, and salt. Stir in the currants, making sure they are separated.

2. Add the buttermilk and mix with a fork to form a soft dough. Sprinkle about ¼ cup of the remaining flour on a work surface, turn the dough out, and knead it until it is smooth, about 5 minutes. Use only as much of the remaining flour as needed to prevent the dough from sticking.

3. Shape the dough into a smooth, round loaf and press it into the prepared skillet. With a single-edge razor blade or a very sharp knife, cut a cross ½ inch deep across the top of the dough.

4. Bake the loaf 1 hour, or until it is lightly browned. It will sound hollow when it is tapped on the top. Remove the bread from the skillet. Rub the top with butter and sprinkle it with 1 teaspoon sugar. Cool it on a wire rack.

Steamed Brown Bread

Colonists discovered that by mixing baking soda with cornmeal, rye and whole-wheat flours, a reasonably light bread could be made. Traditionally called Boston Brown Bread, this was a Saturday night accompaniment to Boston Baked Beans.

MAKES 2 LOAVES

> 1 cup yellow cornmeal
> 1 cup rye flour
> 1 cup whole-wheat flour
> 2 teaspoons baking soda
> 1 teaspoon salt
> 2 cups buttermilk
> ¾ cup dark molasses
> ¾ cup dark seedless raisins

1. Grease two empty 1-pound metal coffee cans. In a large bowl, combine the cornmeal, flours, baking soda, and salt.

2. In a large bowl, with an electric mixer on medium-speed, beat the buttermilk and molasses until they are well blended. Add the flour mixture gradually, beating well after each addition. Stir in the raisins. Spoon the batter evenly into the greased cans. Cover each loosely with a piece of buttered waxed paper, then with a large piece of aluminum foil. Tie both securely to the can with string.

3. Place the cans on a wire rack set in a large saucepot and add enough boiling water to reach halfway up the cans. Over high heat, return the water to boiling. Reduce to low heat; cover and simmer 2¼ hours, adding more boiling water if needed to keep it at a halfway mark on the cans.

4. To serve the bread immediately, remove the foil and paper from the cans. Turn the loaves out onto a cutting board; slice and serve with butter, if desired. Or leave bread in cans with foil and paper intact, and refrigerate for up to 1 week. To reheat, steam it as above just until heated through, about 30 minutes.

Baking Note

The main leavening agents in quick breads and muffins are baking powder and baking soda, which must be fresh to work. If it has been on the shelf for a while, test your ingredient by combining 1 teaspoon with ⅓ cup hot water. If it bubbles actively, it's fresh. Still, it's often helpful to mark the date on the container when it's opened.

Cracklin' Bread

Cracklings are bits of pork fat that have been fried until most of the fat has been rendered out and they are crispy and flavorful. Their addition to this traditional cornbread gives it a light, smoky flavor.

MAKES ONE 9-INCH ROUND LOAF

> ¼ **pound pork fat**
> 1 **cup yellow cornmeal**
> 1 **cup all-purpose flour**
> 1 **teaspoon baking soda**
> ½ **teaspoon salt**
> ¼ **teaspoon ground black pepper**
> 1 **large egg**
> 1½ **cups buttermilk**

1. Cut the pork fat into ¼-inch cubes. In a 9-inch cast-iron skillet, cook the cubes over medium heat until the fat renders out and the cracklings are crisp. Drain the cracklings thoroughly on paper towels. Reserve 2 tablespoons fat from the skillet; discard the rest. Do not wipe out the skillet; just set it aside.

2. Heat the oven to 400°F. In a large bowl, combine the cornmeal, flour, baking soda, salt, and pepper. In another bowl, lightly beat the egg with a fork, then stir in the buttermilk and the reserved fat. Pour the buttermilk mixture over the cornmeal mixture and stir just until the batter is smooth.

3. Pour the batter into the greased skillet. Bake the bread 20 minutes, or until the top is golden brown and the bread has begun to draw away from the edge of the skillet. Cut the bread into wedges and serve warm.

Yeast Breads

Home-baked bread speaks to us of the warmth of the hearth and home. It conjures up bustling kitchens, flour-dusted work counters, large bowls covered with dish-towels, ovens yearning for bread pans filled with plump, yielding dough. The baked bread, which permeates the house with its indescribable aroma, is beautifully browned, its crust crisp or softly elastic. There it sits, cooling on a wire rack, waiting for the time to be right to slice it and spread it with pale creamery butter and maybe a spoonful of strawberry jam.

Making bread is a comfortable task. All it takes is time and warmth: time to knead the dough sufficiently so that the gluten develops and time for the dough to rise once or, usually, twice. Warm water activates the yeast, a warm kitchen helps the dough rise, and a hot oven bakes the bread. Never hesitate to knead the dough for as long as it requires to develop the gluten, gathering it to you as, almost in the same movement, you push it away.

Flour, liquid, and leavener are the basic ingredients in bread making. Most often the flour is all-purpose or bread flour. Both are high in protein, which means they have a good percentage of gluten. Gluten is crucial because as it develops, its strands trap carbon dioxide, and the gas causes the bread to rise. These high-gluten white flours are usually added to whole-wheat or rye flour to prevent a loaf from being dense, low, and heavy. Yeast-raised breads freeze very well and so it is a good idea to make several loaves at one time.

Water is the most common liquid added to bread dough. Some soft-textured breads call for a measure of milk, buttermilk, or yogurt. Still others employ fruit juice, honey, and molasses.

Yeast leavens bread. Packaged dry yeast is the sort we use most often when making yeast bread, although rapid-rising dry yeast works very well in some recipes. Fresh compressed yeast, once the most popular type, is out of favor since it keeps for only two weeks and very few of us bake often enough to make it useful.

Almost every recipe for yeast-raised bread instructs the baker to "proof" or dissolve the yeast in warm water to test the potency of the yeast. The warmth activates the yeast and the resulting bubbles and foam let us know that it is still capable of raising the bread. (You have kept the package of yeast in the refrigerator, but it may not be potent. Check the stamped date before attempting to proof the yeast.) A little sugar may be added to the proofing water—which should be warmer than 105° but cooler than 115°F—to give the yeast something to feed on and so activate a little faster. Yeast doughs require at least one rising, in a warm place, away from drafts.

Bread can be baked in all sizes and shapes . . . free form, round, and braids or coils, and in loaf pans. The standard pan is 9- by 5-inches; all others are specified in the recipe.

Although any number of bakeries carry good bread and much of the packaged sort in the supermarkets is quite tasty, nothing will ever beat home-baked. It fills so many needs besides the obvious one of nourishment. The mixing, kneading, punching down, and patting bring pleasure to the baker, the baking envelops the kitchen in a tantalizing smell, and the finished product tastes so good we almost always go back for more.

Daily Bread

(Photograph, page 41)

Nutritionists say we should eat more whole-grain bread because its high fiber content aids in the prevention of many diseases. This humble but flavorful loaf certainly fills the bill: Its mild flavor works well for breakfast toast and hearty sandwiches.

MAKES 1 LOAF

> 4 to 4¼ cups whole-wheat flour
> 1 package rapid-rising dry yeast
> 1½ teaspoons salt
> 1¾ cups very warm water (120° to 130°F)
> 1 tablespoon vegetable oil
> 1 large egg white
> 1 teaspoon water
> 1 teaspoon sesame seeds
> 1 teaspoon sunflower seeds

1. In the large bowl of an electric mixer on low speed, beat together 3 cups flour, the yeast, and salt. Add the warm water and oil; beat until a soft dough forms. With a wooden spoon, stir in enough remaining flour, about ¾ cup, to make a stiff dough. Turn the dough onto a lightly floured surface.

2. Lightly oil a large bowl; set aside. Knead the dough, working in more flour if necessary, until it is smooth and elastic, 5 to 10 minutes. Shape the dough into a ball and place it in the bowl, turning to bring the oiled side up. Cover with a clean cloth. Let the dough rise in a warm place, away from drafts, until it is double in size, about 35 to 45 minutes.

3. Grease a loaf pan. Punch down the dough. Shape it into an 8- by 4-inch oval, and place in the greased pan. Cover the dough with a clean cloth and let it rise again until it is double in size, about 20 minutes.

4. Heat the oven to 400°F. In a cup, beat the egg white with water and brush it over the top of the loaf. Sprinkle with sesame and sunflower seeds. Bake the loaf 30 to 35 minutes, or until it sounds hollow when tapped on top. Remove it from the pan and cool on a wire rack.

Country White Bread

How long has it been since you've baked a loaf of basic white bread? Try this simple recipe; nothing beats it for morning toast spread with the preserves you put up last summer.

MAKES 1 LOAF

> 1 package active dry yeast
> 1½ cups warm water (105° to 115°F)
> ¼ cup sugar
> 5½ cups all-purpose flour
> 3 tablespoons butter or margarine, softened
> 1 teaspoon salt

1. In a large bowl, sprinkle the yeast over ½ cup warm water. Stir in the sugar and let the mixture stand until foamy, about 10 minutes.

2. Add the remaining 1 cup warm water, 4 cups flour, the butter, and salt to the yeast mixture. Beat with a wooden spoon until smooth. Stir in enough flour to make a manageable dough. Turn the dough onto a lightly floured surface.

3. Lightly oil a large bowl; set aside. Knead the dough, working in more flour if necessary, until it is smooth and elastic, 5 to 10 minutes. Shape the dough into a ball and place it in the bowl, turning to bring the oiled side up. Cover with a clean cloth. Let the dough rise in a warm place, away from drafts, until it is double in size, about 45 minutes.

4. Grease a loaf pan. Punch down the dough. Shape it into an 8- by 4-inch oval, and place in the greased pan. Cover the dough with a clean cloth and let it rise again until it is double in size, 45 to 60 minutes.

5. Heat the oven to 350°F. Bake the loaf 50 to 60 minutes, or until it sounds hollow when tapped on top. Remove it from the pan and cool on a wire rack.

Anadama Bread

New England is the birthplace of this delightful molasses-flavored cornmeal yeast bread.

MAKES 2 LOAVES

> 2 cups water
> ½ cup yellow cornmeal
> ¼ cup (½ stick) butter or margarine
> ½ cup dark molasses
> 1½ teaspoons salt
> 1 package active dry yeast
> ½ cup warm water (105° to 115°F)
> 5 cups all-purpose flour

1. In a heavy 1-quart saucepan, heat 1½ cups water to boiling. In a small bowl, combine the cornmeal and remaining ½ cup water. Stir the cornmeal mixture into the boiling water. Cook, stirring, until the mixture is thickened and bubbly, and allow to boil 1 minute. Remove from the heat. Beat in the butter, molasses, and salt. Cool to warm.

2. In a large bowl, sprinkle the yeast over the warm water; stir and set aside to soften, about 5 minutes. Add the cornmeal mixture to the yeast mixture; mix well. With a wooden spoon, beat in 4 cups flour, ½ cup at a time. Stir in enough flour to make a manageable dough. Turn the dough onto a lightly floured surface.

3. Lightly oil a large bowl; set aside. Knead the dough, working in more flour if necessary, until it is smooth and elastic, 5 to 10 minutes. Shape the dough into a ball and place it in the bowl, turning to bring the oiled side up. Cover with a clean cloth. Let the dough rise in a warm place, away from drafts, until it is double in size, about 1½ hours.

4. Grease 2 loaf pans. Punch down the dough and cut it in half. Shape each half into an 8-by 4-inch oval; place one oval in each greased pan. Cover the dough with a clean cloth and let it rise again until it is double in size, about 1 hour.

5. Heat the oven to 400°F. Bake the loaves 45 to 55 minutes, or until they sound hollow when tapped on top. Remove them from the pans and cool on wire racks.

Breadmaking Note

One package of active dry yeast contains 2 teaspoons and equals one .6-ounce cake of fresh compressed yeast.

French Bread

(Photograph, page 42)

Frenchmen will tell you that no where in the world can their light, airy, irresistible bread be made but in the brick ovens of France. True, the flour, the yeast—even the water—are different in Europe. Yet we have developed a recipe using beer (for the malty flavor supplied in other recipes by brewer's yeast) and cake flour (for a softer dough).

MAKES 2 LOAVES

> 1 package active dry yeast
> ½ cup warm water (105° to 115°F)
> 2½ to 3 cups all-purpose flour
> 1 cup cake flour
> ¾ cup beer, at room temperature
> 1 teaspoon salt
> 1 tablespoon cornmeal
> ¼ teaspoon salt
> ¼ cup water

1. In a large bowl, sprinkle the yeast over the warm water. Stir and set aside to soften, about 5 minutes.

2. Add 2 cups all-purpose flour, the cake flour, beer, and ¾ teaspoon salt to the yeast mixture. Beat with a wooden spoon until smooth, then beat for about 4 minutes. Stir in just enough all-purpose flour to stiffen the dough slightly, about ½ cup. (The dough will be softer than other bread dough.)

3. Turn the dough out onto a lightly floured surface. Let it rest about 3 minutes.

4. Lightly oil a large bowl; set aside. Knead the dough, using a pastry scraper, by scraping under one side of the dough and lifting to fold the dough over itself. Repeat the folding process from alternate sides, working rapidly, for about 2 minutes, until the dough changes texture and becomes more elastic. Knead the dough 5 minutes more.

5. Shape the dough into a ball and place it in the bowl, turning to bring the oiled side up. Cover with a clean cloth. Let the dough rise at room temperature, away from drafts, until it is double in size, about 1½ hours.

6. Sprinkle a large baking sheet with the cornmeal. Turn the dough out onto a lightly floured surface and divide it in half. Shape each half into a ball and let it rest about 4 minutes. Pat one ball into a 9-inch oval. Fold the oval in half lengthwise; seal the edge, and flatten again. Fold the dough lengthwise and seal the edge; turn the dough sealed-side down. With your palms, roll the dough back and forth to form a rope about 16 inches long. Lift the rope onto the prepared baking sheet. Repeat the process with the remaining dough.

7. Cover the loaves with a clean cloth and let them rise again until they are almost triple in volume, about 1½ hours.

8. Set one oven rack at the lowest level of the oven and one at middle. Heat the oven to 450°F. In a cup, dissolve the remaining ¼ teaspoon salt in the water. With a single-edge razor blade, make 3 diagonal slashes across the top of each loaf. Lightly brush the loaves with salt water. Place the baking sheet on the lowest rack of the oven. Bake 10 minutes. Move the sheet to the middle rack and brush the loaves with salt water again. Bake another 10 minutes, or until the loaves are lightly browned and crusty. The bread will sound hollow when tapped on the top. Turn off the oven and let the loaves remain in oven 8 minutes. Remove them from the baking sheet and cool on a wire rack.

Cheesy Wheat Bread

Enriched with whole-wheat flour, textured with bulgur, and flavored with nearly two cups of sharp farmhouse Cheddar, Cheesy Wheat Bread is a particularly healthful bread to serve your family.

MAKES 1 LOAF

> 2 cups all-purpose flour
> 1¼ cups whole-wheat flour
> ¼ cup bulgur
> 1 package rapid-rising dry yeast
> 1 teaspoon salt
> 1 teaspoon brown sugar
> 1½ cups very warm water (120° to 130°F)
> 1 tablespoon butter, melted
> 1¾ cups (7 ounces) shredded sharp
>   Cheddar cheese

1. In the large bowl of an electric mixer, combine 1 cup all-purpose flour, 1 cup whole-wheat flour, the bulgur, yeast, salt, sugar, water, and butter. With the mixer on low speed, beat just until the dry ingredients are moistened. With a wooden spoon, beat in the remaining all-purpose and wheat flours. The dough will be sticky.

2. Cover the bowl with a clean cloth. Let the dough rise in a warm place, away from drafts, until it is double in size, 35 to 45 minutes.

3. Grease an 8-inch round baking pan. Stir down the dough, then stir in 1 cup cheese. Turn the dough onto a lightly floured surface. With a floured rolling pin, roll the dough to an 18- by 8-inch rectangle. Place the rectangle so that its short edge faces you. Lightly mark the long edges of the dough into thirds.

Sprinkle nearly half of the remaining cheese over the center third of the dough. Fold the bottom third of the dough over the center and sprinkle it with most of the remaining cheese. Fold over the top third of the dough. Pat the dough around the edges to seal in the cheese. Coil the dough to fit in the greased pan.

4. Cover the dough with a clean cloth and let it rise again until it is double in size, about 1¼ hours.

5. Heat the oven to 400°F. Sprinkle the loaf with the remaining cheese. Bake the loaf 35 minutes, or until it sounds hollow when tapped on the top. Remove it from the pan and cool on a wire rack.

Breadmaking Note

Store breads in a cool, dry place, tightly wrapped in plastic wrap or enclosed in a plastic bag. Storing breads in the refrigerator will retard molding, but the bread will become stale. Tightly-wrapped bread will keep in the freezer up to three months.

Swirled Cinnamon Raisin Bread

(Photograph, page 59)

Slice this rounded loaf and discover a sweet cinnamon filling nestled in the curves of the dough. It's just fine to eat plain, but do try it with Apple Butter (page 179).

MAKES 1 LOAF

> 1 package active dry yeast
> 1½ cups warm water (105° to 115°F)
> 5½ cups all-purpose flour
> 1 teaspoon salt
> ⅓ cup sugar
> 3 tablespoons butter or margarine, softened
> 1 teaspoon ground cinnamon
> ½ cup dark seedless raisins

1. In a small bowl, sprinkle the yeast over ½ cup of water. Stir and set aside to soften, about 5 minutes. In a large bowl, combine 5 cups flour and the salt. Set aside 2 tablespoons sugar. Stir the remaining sugar into the flour mixture.

2. Add the yeast mixture, remaining 1 cup water, and the butter to the flour mixture. Stir with a wooden spoon until all ingredients are moistened. Knead the dough in the bowl until it forms a ball.

3. Sprinkle a board or work surface with the remaining ½ cup flour. Turn the dough onto the board and knead it until it is smooth and elastic, 3 to 5 minutes.

4. Lightly oil a large bowl; set aside. Shape the dough into a ball and place it in the bowl, turning to bring the oiled side up. Cover with a clean cloth. Let the dough rise in a warm place, away from drafts, until it is double in size, about 45 minutes.

5. Grease and flour a loaf pan. Punch down the dough. Roll it to a 12- by 8-inch rectangle and turn it over.

6. Lightly brush the dough with water. Stir the cinnamon into the remaining 2 tablespoons sugar and sprinkle over the dough. Top with the raisins. Starting from a short side, roll the dough up, jelly-roll style, pinching to seal the outside edge. Fit the dough into the prepared pan, seam-side down.

7. Cover the dough with a clean cloth and let it rise again until it is double in size, 45 to 60 minutes.

8. Heat the oven to 350°F. Bake the bread 50 to 60 minutes, or until it is golden brown. It will sound hollow when tapped on the top. Remove it from the pan and cool on a wire rack.

Country Pumpernickel

Molasses, cocoa, and rye flour give this loaf its dense, dark goodness. Pumpernickel is cold weather bread, best served with robust meats and mustards, but also good on a frigid, snowy morning toasted and topped with Rich Homemade Cream Cheese (page 180) and Farmhouse Ginger Marmalade (page 174).

MAKES 1 LARGE LOAF OR 1 DOZEN ROLLS

> 2 packages active dry yeast
> 1½ cups warm water (105° to 115°F)
> ½ cup dark molasses
> 3 cups rye flour
> ⅓ cup unsweetened cocoa powder
> 2 tablespoons caraway seeds
> ¼ cup vegetable shortening
> 1 teaspoon salt
> 2 to 2½ cups all-purpose flour
> ½ cup dark seedless raisins (optional)
> 2 to 3 tablespoons yellow cornmeal
> Additional caraway seeds (optional)

1. In a large bowl, sprinkle the yeast over the warm water. Stir in the molasses and let the mixture stand until foamy, about 10 minutes.

2. Add the rye flour, cocoa, caraway seeds, shortening, and salt to the yeast mixture. Beat the batter with a wooden spoon until it is smooth. Stir in enough all-purpose flour to make a manageable dough. Turn the dough onto a lightly floured surface.

3. Lightly oil a large bowl; set aside. Knead the dough, working in more flour if necessary, until it is smooth and elastic, 5 to 10 minutes. Knead in the raisins, if desired. Shape the dough into a ball.

4. Place the dough in the bowl, turning to bring the oiled side up. Cover with a clean cloth. Let the dough rise in a warm place, away from drafts, until it is double in size, about 1 hour. Punch down the dough and let it rise until double again, about 20 minutes.

5. Grease a baking sheet and sprinkle it with cornmeal. Punch down the dough. Shape it into a round loaf or 12 rolls. Place the dough on the greased sheet. Score the top of the loaf with a knife or the tines of a fork; sprinkle with additional caraway seeds, if desired. Cover the dough with a clean cloth and let it rise again until it is double in size, about 40 minutes.

6. Heat the oven to 375°F. Bake the loaf 30 to 35 minutes or the rolls 15 to 20 minutes, until the bread sounds hollow when tapped on the top. Remove the loaf or rolls from the baking sheet and cool on a wire rack.

Breadmaking Note

To vary the appearance of your homemade bread, sprinkle the tops with sesame or poppy seeds, wheat germ, sugar, or spices. Or, for a shiny surface, brush the unbaked bread with an egg beaten with a tablespoon of water.

Bagels

(Photograph, page 155)

Believed to have originated in Poland or Germany, the bagel has been thoroughly assimilated into the American way of life. Many cooks are intimidated by the prospect of making their own bagels, but the process is really quite easy to master. The secret is to boil the bagels briefly before they are baked. Here we include variations: egg, rye, whole-wheat, pumpernickel raisin, and salt-free. Once baked and cooled, bagels can be frozen; to serve, reheat them, loosely covered with aluminum foil, in a 400°F oven for 10 minutes.

MAKES 8 BAGELS

> 1 package active dry yeast
> 1½ cups warm water (105° to 115°F)
> 2 tablespoons sugar
> 3½ to 4 cups bread flour
> 2 teaspoons salt

TOPPING:
> Poppy-seeds, sesame seeds, coarse
>   salt, instant minced onion, or instant
>   minced garlic

1.   In a large bowl, sprinkle the yeast over the water. Stir in 1 tablespoon sugar and set aside until foamy, about 10 minutes.

2.   Add 3½ cups flour and 1 teaspoon salt to the yeast mixture. Stir rapidly with a fork until all the flour has been moistened. Knead the dough in the bowl until it forms a ball. Let it rest 15 minutes.

3.   Lightly oil a large bowl; set aside. Turn the dough out onto a lightly floured surface. Knead it, adding only as much of the remaining ½ cup flour as necessary to keep it from sticking, until it is smooth and elastic, about 8 minutes. Shape the dough into a ball and place it in the bowl, turning to bring the oiled side up. Cover the dough with a clean cloth and let it rise in a warm place, away from drafts, until it is double in size, about 30 minutes.

4.   Divide the dough into 8 pieces. Shape each into a ball and flatten it with the palm of your hand. With a finger, poke a hole in the center of each bagel and stretch to make the hole about 1 inch in diameter. Lightly moisten a baking sheet with water, and arrange the bagels on the sheet.

5.   Cover the bagels with a clean cloth and let them rise again until they are double in size, 50 to 60 minutes.

6.   Heat the oven to 475°F. In a medium-size skillet, heat 1 quart water to boiling. Add the remaining 1 tablespoon sugar and 1 teaspoon salt. Add the bagels, several at a time, and boil 1 minute. Turn them and boil 1 minute longer.

7.   Place a moistened cotton or linen kitchen towel on a baking sheet. With a slotted spatula, transfer the bagels to the towel. Bake 5 minutes.

8.   Remove the bagels from the oven. Turn the bagels over onto an ungreased baking sheet (without a towel). Sprinkle them with a topping, if desired. Bake the bagels 20 to 25 minutes longer, or until they are golden brown and sound hollow when gently tapped. Serve warm or at room temperature.

Egg Bagels

Reduce water to 1¼ cups. Beat 1 large egg and add to the yeast mixture along with the flour.

Pumpernickel Raisin Bagels

Use 1¼ cups water in place of 1½ cups water. Replace 1 cup bread flour with 1 cup rye flour. Stir 1 1-ounce square unsweetened chocolate, melted, 2 tablespoons molasses, 2 teaspoons caraway seeds, and ¼ cup dark seedless raisins into the yeast mixture just before adding the flour.

Rye Bagels

Replace 1 cup bread flour with 1 cup rye flour. Mix in 2 teaspoons caraway seeds when adding the flour mixture.

Salt-free Bagels

Replace the 1 teaspoon salt in the flour mixture with 1 teaspoon salt-free, 14-herb-and-spice blend. Eliminate the salt in the boiling water.

Whole-wheat Bagels

Reduce bread flour to 1½ cups and add 1½ cups whole-wheat flour. Whole-wheat bagels may take a few minutes more to bake.

Baking Bread

Baking Bread—it's an act of creation. Bread literally grows from your hands. You bring the dormant yeast to life, knead the flour into a dough, nurture it, care for it, and shape it into a loaf, then bake it until it's golden brown and smooth outside, chewy and light inside.

Bread baking is one of the most ancient, most elemental rituals. Before there were molds, loaves were usually round. Before there were ovens, dough was flattened for easier cooking. Today, round and flat loaves are still popular, but breads come in all shapes and sizes, and from all kinds of grains. Sardinian bakers make very thin crackling rounds called "fogli di musica" (sheets of music); from France we get long, crusty baguettes; in Mexico tortillas are most popular; and the Portuguese are known for their light, puffy sweet bread.

Every bread has a unique history. The American bread sold commercially today has its roots in a frontier society in which flour mills were few and far between; imperishable products were valued. Wheat, once crushed, does not keep well; the oil in the germ spoils and the flour attracts weevils. Bolting—to remove the germ and bran—became popular. But yeast doesn't thrive in flour bereft of germ, and so early American bakers began adding sugar to the dough, to hurry the rising process along. American breads became sweeter and puffier—and less nutritious.

This is one reason baking bread at home is becoming popular again. Today there is a new emphasis on natural flours, with which you can make your own wholesome loaves and ensure your family's health. After all, there's nothing as basic, as nourishing, and as honestly satisfying as a slice of warm, buttered, freshly baked bread.

Whole-wheat Raisin Loaves

Few foods are better in the morning than toasted raisin bread spread with melting sweet butter. The whole-wheat flour in this bread adds body and flavor, but the dough has an almost equal measure of all-purpose flour to keep it light.

MAKES 2 LOAVES

> 1½ **cups milk**
> ¼ **cup honey**
> ½ **cup (1 stick) butter or margarine, softened**
> 2 **packages active dry yeast**
> ½ **cup warm water (105° to 115°F)**
> 2 **large eggs**
> 3 **cups whole-wheat flour**
> 1½ **teaspoons ground cinnamon**
> 1 **teaspoon salt**
> 3 to 3½ **cups all-purpose flour**
> 2 **cups dark seedless raisins**
> 1 **large egg white**
> 2 **tablespoons water**

1. In a 1-quart saucepan, combine the milk and honey. Over medium heat, heat the milk until bubbles form around the side of the pan, then remove from the heat. Stir in the butter. Cool to warm.

2. In a large bowl, preferably of a heavy-duty electric mixer, sprinkle the yeast over the warm water. Stir and set aside to soften, about 5 minutes.

3. Add the milk mixture and the eggs to the yeast mixture. Beat on low speed until well mixed. Add the whole-wheat flour, cinnamon, and salt. Beat until smooth. Gradually beat in enough all-purpose flour to make a soft dough. Knead the dough, either manually or with the mixer's dough hook, until it is smooth and elastic, adding as much of the remaining flour as necessary. (Hand mixing will require more flour.)

4. Lightly oil a large bowl. Shape the dough into a ball and place it in the bowl, turning to bring the oiled side up. Cover the bowl with a clean cloth. Let the dough rise in a warm place, away from drafts, until it is double in size, about 45 minutes.

5. Punch down the dough and knead in the raisins. Return it to the bowl and cover with a cloth. Let it rise again until it is double in size, about 45 minutes.

6. Grease two 8½- by 4½-inch loaf pans. Punch down the dough. Turn it onto a floured surface and cut it in half. Shape each half into a ball; let them rest 5 minutes. Roll each half into a 9- by 5-inch rectangle. Starting from a long side, roll the dough up, jelly-roll style, pinching to seal the outside edge. Fit them into the greased pans, seam sides down.

7. Cover the breads with a cloth. Let them rise again until they are double in size, 35 to 45 minutes.

8. Heat the oven to 375°F. In a cup, beat the egg white and water. Brush the egg wash on the loaves. Bake the breads 30 to 35 minutes, or until they are golden brown. The bread will sound hollow when tapped on the top. If the loaves brown too much after 25 minutes, cover them with aluminum foil. Remove the loaves from the pans and cool on wire racks.

(Overleaf)
Corned Beef Hash with Eggs, recipe page 106
Grilled Sticky Buns, recipe page 131

Swirled Cinnamon Raisin Bread, page 54   *Lancaster County Breakfast Cheese, page 181*

Apple Butter, page 179

Cinnamon-Raisin French Toast, page 71

Brioche

Rich in butter and eggs, brioche is said to have originated centuries ago in Brie, and to have been flavored with the cheese for which this area of France is noted. Our interpretation is made without the cheese.

MAKES 1 LOAF OR 8 ROLLS

> ¾ cup (1½ sticks) butter or
> margarine, softened
> ½ cup milk
> 2 tablespoons sugar
> 1 teaspoon salt
> 4 to 4½ cups all-purpose flour
> 1 package active dry yeast
> 4 large eggs
> 1 teaspoon water

1. In a 1-quart saucepan, combine the butter, milk, sugar, and salt. Heat over medium heat just until the butter melts. Cool to very warm.

2. In a large bowl, combine 2 cups flour and the yeast. Add the butter mixture. With an electric mixer at medium speed, beat the mixture 1 minute. Separate 1 egg and add the white to the flour mixture, reserving the yolk in a cup with the water.

3. Beat the remaining 3 whole eggs into the flour mixture until well mixed. Reduce the mixer speed to low; beat in 1½ cups flour to form a soft dough. Sprinkle the remaining flour on a board and turn the dough onto the board.

4. Lightly oil a large bowl; set aside. Knead the dough, working in more flour if necessary, until it is smooth and elastic, 5 to 10 minutes. Shape the dough into a ball and place it in the bowl, turning to bring the oiled side up. Cover with a clean cloth. Let the dough rise in a warm place, away from drafts, until it is double in size, about 1½ hours.

5. Grease a 6-cup brioche mold (about 10-inches across the top) or eight 3-inch individual brioche molds. Punch down the dough.

For a large brioche, pinch off a 3-inch-piece of dough and shape into a small ball. Shape the remaining dough into a large ball; place it in the greased mold. Make an indentation in the center of the large ball. Moisten the bottom of the small ball with water and fit it into the indentation of the large ball. Cover the dough with a clean cloth and let it rise again until it is double in size, about 1 hour.

To make individual brioches, divide the dough into 8 pieces. Shape each piece into 1 large ball and 1 small ball. Place the large balls into the greased molds. Make an indentation in the center of each. Moisten the bottom of each small ball; place it into the indentation of a larger ball. Cover the dough with a clean cloth and let it rise again, about 45 minutes.

6. Heat the oven to 325°F for the large brioche or 350°F for the rolls. Beat the egg yolk and water slightly; brush some over the brioche or rolls. (Do not discard the remaining egg wash.) Bake the brioche 35 to 40 minutes or the rolls 15 to 20 minutes, until the bread is golden brown and firm.

7. Remove the brioche from the oven and immediately brush again with the remaining egg wash. Remove the brioche or rolls from the mold(s) and cool completely on a wire rack.

Sourdough Bread

With its tangy flavor, dense texture, and hearty crust, sourdough bread is enjoying a renewed popularity across America. Made from a naturally fermented starter, sourdough was the bread of the pioneers, who were rarely able to get fresh yeast.

MAKES 1 LARGE OR 2 SMALL ROUND LOAVES

> **SOURDOUGH STARTER:**
> 1 package active dry yeast
> 1½ cups warm water (105° to 115°F)
> 1 tablespoon sugar
> 1½ cups all-purpose flour
>
> 1 package active dry yeast
> 1¾ cups warm water (105° to 115°F)
> 1 tablespoon sugar
> 6½ to 7 cups all-purpose flour
> 1½ teaspoons salt
> ¼ teaspoon baking soda

1. Three or four days before making bread, prepare the Sourdough Starter: In a medium-size bowl, sprinkle the yeast over the warm water. Stir in the sugar and let the mixture stand until foamy, about 10 minutes. Stir in the flour until the mixture is smooth. Cover and set aside at room temperature overnight. Then refrigerate the starter until you are ready to use it, at least three more days, stirring once a day. When some of the starter is used, replace with ½ cup flour, ½ cup warm water, and 1 teaspoon sugar for each cup removed.

2. To make the bread, in a large bowl, sprinkle the yeast over the warm water. Stir in the sugar and let the mixture stand until foamy, about 10 minutes.

3. Add 1 cup starter, 5 cups flour, the salt, and baking soda to the yeast mixture. Beat with a wooden spoon until the mixture is smooth. Stir in enough flour to make a manageable dough. Turn the dough onto a lightly floured surface.

4. Lightly oil a large bowl; set aside. Knead the dough, working in more flour if necessary, until it is smooth and elastic, 5 to 10 minutes. Shape the dough into a ball and place it in the bowl, turning to bring the oiled side up. Cover with a clean cloth. Let the dough rise in a warm place, away from drafts, until it is double in size, about 45 minutes.

5. Grease a large baking sheet. Punch down the dough. Shape it into one large round loaf or divide it in half and shape each into a round loaf. Place the dough on the greased sheet. With a single-edge razor blade make 3 slashes across the top of each loaf. Cover the dough with a clean cloth and let it rise again until it is double in size, about 45 to 60 minutes.

6. Heat the oven to 400°F. Bake the bread 25 to 35 minutes, or until it sounds hollow when tapped on the top. Remove it from the baking sheet and cool on a wire rack.

Breadmaking Note

Making your own sourdough starter is an easy proposition and if refrigerated, it will keep for months in a lidded glass or ceramic container. It is a good idea to scoop the starter from the container about once a month, set it aside, and wash the container thoroughly before returning the starter to it.

Rusks

Gently flavored and slightly sweet, rusks are a subtle temptation. Served with homemade Hot Chocolate (page 186) or Café au Lait (page 187), they are reminiscent of leisurely European breakfast. Our airy, golden version is lovely as a late evening snack, too.

MAKES 4 DOZEN RUSKS

> ¾ cup milk
> 2 tablespoons butter or margarine
> 1 package active dry yeast
> ½ cup warm water (105° to 115°F)
> 4½ to 5 cups all-purpose flour
> ¼ cup sugar
> ¾ teaspoon salt
> 3 large eggs

1. In a 1-quart saucepan, heat the milk until bubbles form around the side of the pan. Remove from the heat. Stir in the butter and cool to warm.

2. In a small bowl, sprinkle the yeast over the water; stir and set aside to soften, about 5 minutes. In a large bowl, combine 4½ cups flour, the sugar, and salt.

3. Add the warm milk mixture to the flour mixture, along with the softened yeast and the eggs. Stir with a wooden spoon until the ingredients are well combined. Knead the dough in the bowl until it forms a ball.

4. Turn the dough out onto a lightly floured board. Knead it until it is smooth and shiny, about 5 minutes. Add the remaining flour, if necessary, to make a manageable dough.

5. Lightly oil a large bowl. Shape the dough into a ball and place it in the bowl, turning to bring the oiled side up. Cover the dough with a clean cloth and let it rise in a warm place, away from drafts, until it is double in size, about 45 minutes.

6. Punch down the dough. Lightly grease 2 baking sheets. Divide the dough into quarters. Shape these into ½-inch-thick ovals on the greased baking sheets. Cover the dough with a clean cloth and let it rise again until it is double in size, about 45 minutes.

7. Heat the oven to 375°F. Bake the loaves 15 to 20 minutes, or until they are golden. Remove them from the baking sheets and cool completely on wire racks.

8. With a very sharp knife, cut the ovals crosswise into ½-inch-thick slices. Arrange the slices on ungreased baking sheets. Heat the oven to 275°F. Bake the rusks 20 to 25 minutes, or until they are golden. Turn and bake the other sides 20 to 25 minutes longer.

9. Cool the rusks completely on wire racks and store them in an airtight container.

Breadmaking Note

Dough is double in size when a finger pressed into it leaves a dent that remains. Dough containing low-gluten flours or cornmeal will take longer to rise than dough made from all-purpose flour.

Toast, Pancakes & Waffles

A healthy stack of pancakes on a big plate, a pitcher of warmed syrup and a few pats of sweet butter mean breakfast—a hearty, filling breakfast to prepare us for a day at work, in school, or out at the woodpile splitting logs.

Fresh eggs, a jug of milk, and a loaf of bread can be turned into a morning meal that ranks high when it comes to breakfast favorites. Known as French toast in this country, the actual French version is called *pain perdue*. This translates to mean "lost bread," probably so called because this pan-fried meal is a good way to use up day-old or nearly stale bread that otherwise would be discarded. As good as French toast is with any slice of bread, try making it with homemade. There is no need to smother this culinary treat with syrup or honey, although you may if that is your preference. Simply spoon some crème fraîche or fresh fruit over the hot-from-the-skillet bread.

Pancakes are called all sorts of names, from griddle cakes to flapjacks and frycakes. All are made from a sweetened milk-and-egg batter, fried into shape on a hot griddle or in a hot skillet, and served from stove to plate with syrup, honey, jam, or a sprinkling of sugar.

The batter can be made a few days in advance and refrigerated for spur-of-the-moment cooking, but once the cakes are fried, it is best to eat them right away. If you stack them and try to hold them in a warm oven, they will weigh themselves down and turn soggy.

As popular as pancakes are, waffles are equally loved when it comes time for breakfast. Who can resist a crisp, golden waffle, its pockets brimming with amber-colored syrup? The face and shape of waffle irons may have changed with time, but our affection for wholesome, fresh, homemade waffles remains constant.

The way to a perfect waffle is by trial and error. Experimenting is the only way to attain a waffle of perfect color and texture, but there are a few helpful signs to look for. Most waffle irons have a light or dial to indicate when the iron is hot and ready for the batter. Heat your waffle iron according to the directions supplied by its manufacturer. As a general rule, the waffle is done when steam stops escaping from the sides of the iron—usually after three to six minutes. However, if the waffle cannot be lifted from the grid easily, it is not properly cooked. Simply put the lid back on and cook the waffle for another minute.

Bringing the waffle iron to the table is the best way to make waffles. This way, you can fork them directly onto waiting plates and while they are still hot, they can be piled with butter, syrup, honey, or fresh fruit. Or, waffles can be kept warm in a low oven as the others cook. When you take the trouble to make waffles, it is a good idea to bake an extra batch. Let them cool completely and then wrap each waffle in aluminum foil or plastic wrap and freeze them. During the next month or two, take them as you want them from the freezer and pop them in the toaster. They will thaw and heat at the same time and be just as crisp as the day they were made. They will taste far better than the storebought variety of frozen waffles. You can count on that.

French Bread French Toast

In France, bread is bought just-baked from the *boulangerie* twice a day to assure freshness. For delightful as it is, French bread is notoriously quick to stale. And perhaps it is this characteristic that has blessed us with the perfect use for stale bread: French toast. Slice up a loaf of day-old bread and let it soak in the honey-vanilla-flavored egg mixture well ahead of time. This recipe can easily be doubled for a larger gathering.

MAKES 4 TO 5 SERVINGS

> 1 long loaf French bread (about 20 inches
>   long, 3 inches wide)
> 6 large eggs
> 1 cup (½ pint) heavy cream
> ¼ cup honey
> ¼ teaspoon ground nutmeg
> ¼ teaspoon vanilla extract
> 3 tablespoons butter, melted
> ½ pint basket strawberries or other
>   berries, rinsed and dried
> 1 cup maple syrup, warmed

1.   Cut the bread diagonally into 1-inch-thick slices. In a large bowl, beat the eggs, cream, honey, nutmeg, and vanilla until well mixed.

2.   In an 8-inch-square baking dish, place the bread slices. Pour the egg mixture over the bread and turn the slices to coat them evenly. Cover the dish with plastic wrap and refrigerate at least 2 hours or overnight.

3.   Heat the oven to 400°F. Line a 15½-by 10½-inch jelly-roll pan with aluminum foil. Arrange the soaked bread slices in a single layer in the pan. Bake the French toast 15 to 20 minutes, or until it is golden brown, turning once midway through the baking time.

4.   To serve, brush the toast with melted butter and transfer to serving plates; garnish with fresh berries. Pass the maple syrup at the table.

Cinnamon Toast

Cinnamon toast is another dish so simple that you don't really need a recipe.

MAKES 1 SERVING

> 2 slices bread
> 2 teaspoons butter
> 2 teaspoons sugar
> Pinch of ground cinnamon

1.   Heat the broiler. Toast the bread, then spread with butter.

2.   In a cup, mix the sugar with the cinnamon and sprinkle over the buttered side of the toast.

3.   Broil the sugared side of the toast until the sugar melts.

Outrageous French Toast

On family special occasion days—birthdays, anniversaries, graduations—start the celebration with breakfast. There can be few more indulgent breakfasts than this stunningly rich chocolate and pistachio filled French toast. The chocolate you'll need is available in the candy section of your market.

MAKES 6 SERVINGS

> 6 1-inch-thick diagonal slices large Italian
>   or French bread (preferably a day old)
> 1 3-ounce bar semisweet or dark
>   chocolate
> 6 teaspoons chopped unsalted pistachio nuts
> 3 large eggs
> ¾ cup milk
> 2 tablespoons sugar
> 1 teaspoon vanilla extract
> ⅛ teaspoon ground nutmeg
> ¼ cup (½ stick) butter or margarine
> About ¼ cup confectioners' sugar

1. With a serrated knife, cut a pocket horizontally in each slice of bread through the top crust. Cut the candy bar into 6 rectangles. Fill each bread slice with a piece of chocolate and 1 teaspoon pistachios.

2. In a shallow dish or pie plate, whisk together the eggs, milk, sugar, vanilla, and nutmeg.

3. On a griddle or in a large skillet over medium heat, melt and spread 1 tablespoon butter.

4. Dip the filled bread slices, one at a time, into the egg mixture, turning to coat both sides and being careful not to squeeze out the chocolate filling. Cook the slices, several at a time, on the hot griddle until they are browned on both sides. Add more butter as needed. Transfer the French toast to heated plates and dust with confectioners' sugar just before serving.

Old Time Milk Toast

Toast is synonymous with breakfast and mild, soothing milk toast is the ultimate comfort food.

MAKES 1 SERVING

> 2 slices bread
> 2 teaspoons butter
> 1 cup milk
> 1 teaspoon sugar
> Pinch of ground nutmeg

1. Toast the bread, then spread with butter. Place the toast in a bowl.

2. In a 1-quart saucepan, gently heat the milk, sugar, and nutmeg over low heat until the mixture is warm, stirring to dissolve the sugar. Pour the milk over the toast and let the mixture stand until the toast swells up or absorbs the milk.

French Toasted Cranberry Bread Pudding

On lazy winter weekends, we're always glad to have a make-ahead dish for breakfast. This unusual bread pudding and its special syrup are prepared the day before, and all that's left to do at serving time is a quick French-toasting of the pudding slices.

MAKES 6 SERVINGS

> 12 slices firm white bread, cubed
> 1 cup cranberries
> 1 cup coarsely chopped walnuts
> 2½ cups milk
> 6 large eggs
> 1½ cups half-and-half
> ⅓ cup granulated sugar
> 1 tablespoon vanilla extract
> ½ teaspoon ground cinnamon
> ¼ teaspoon ground cloves
>
> **CRANBERRY SYRUP:**
> 2 cups cranberries
> 1½ cups water
> 1 cup sugar
> ⅛ teaspoon ground cloves
>
> ¼ cup (½ stick) butter or margarine

1. The day before serving, prepare the bread pudding. Heat the oven to 350°F. Grease a 9- by 5-inch loaf pan. In the greased pan, combine the bread cubes, cranberries, and walnuts.

2. In a 1-quart saucepan, warm the milk. In a medium-size bowl, lightly beat 4 eggs. Beat in 1 cup half-and-half, the granulated sugar, vanilla, cinnamon, and cloves. Very gradually beat in the warmed milk. Pour the milk mixture over the bread mixture in the loaf pan. Let it stand 5 minutes.

3. Bake the bread pudding 60 to 65 minutes, or until it is firm in the center. Place the pudding on a wire rack and cool to room temperature. Cover and refrigerate overnight.

4. Prepare the Cranberry Syrup: In a small saucepan, combine the cranberries, water, sugar, and cloves. Heat to boiling, stirring until the syrup has thickened and the cranberries pop. Cool the syrup to room temperature. In an electric blender, puree the cranberry syrup. Cover and refrigerate.

5. Just before serving, in a pie plate, beat the remaining 2 eggs and the remaining ½ cup half-and-half. Remove the bread pudding from its pan and cut into 12 slices.

6. In a large skillet, melt 1 tablespoon butter. Dip the bread-pudding slices, one at a time, in the egg mixture, turning to coat both sides. Cook the slices, several at a time, in the hot skillet until they are browned on both sides, adding more butter as needed. Transfer the slices to a baking sheet or tray. Keep them warm in a low oven until all the slices have been fried. Serve the toast with the syrup.

Cinnamon-Raisin French Toast

(Photograph, page 62)

Any French toast is only as good as the bread it is made from, and in this case, the toast is sublime. Thick slices of hearty, homemade whole-wheat raisin bread are dipped in a cinnamon-scented egg bath, cooked in butter, and served with confectioners' sugar and maple syrup.

MAKES 4 TO 6 SERVINGS

> 1 Whole-wheat Raisin Loaf (page 58)
> 4 large eggs
> 1 cup milk
> ½ teaspoon ground cinnamon
> ¼ cup (½ stick) butter or margarine
> ¼ cup confectioners' sugar
> 1 cup maple syrup, warmed

1. At least one day ahead, bake the Whole-wheat Raisin Loaf.

2. Cut the bread into 10 thick slices and set aside.

3. In a shallow dish or a pie plate, beat the eggs, milk, and cinnamon. In a large skillet, melt 1 tablespoon butter. Dip the bread slices, one at a time, into the egg mixture, turning to coat both sides. Cook the slices, several at a time, in the hot skillet until they are browned on both sides, adding more butter as needed.

4. Transfer the toast to a baking sheet or tray to keep warm in a low oven until all slices have been fried. Serve the toast warm, passing it with confectioners' sugar, butter, and maple syrup.

German Pancake

This large, golden puff of a pancake, also called a plantation cake in some regions of the country, is baked in a cast-iron skillet in a very hot oven. It will fall a little as you carry it, still in the skillet, from oven to table, and it should be eaten right away. While it needs only a generous dusting of confectioners' sugar, it is also very good with a variety of toppings, from chopped ham to sautéed apples.

MAKES 1 PANCAKE (2 TO 4 SERVINGS)

> 1 tablespoon butter
> 3 large eggs
> ⅓ cup all-purpose flour
> ⅓ cup milk
> ¼ teaspoon salt
> Confectioners' sugar, for dusting
> Assorted toppings: chopped boiled ham,
>   diced sweet red and green peppers,
>   orange marmalade, sautéed apple slices,
>   and crumbled fried bacon

1. Heat the oven to 450°F. In a heavy 9-inch skillet with an oven-safe handle, melt the butter, tilting the skillet to thoroughly grease the bottom and the side of the pan.

2. In a medium-size bowl, with an electric mixer on medium-high speed, beat the eggs until they are thick and fluffy. Reduce the speed to low and gradually beat in the flour, milk, and salt.

3. Pour the batter into the greased skillet. Bake 20 minutes, or until the pancake puffs and is golden brown.

4. Dust the pancake with confectioners' sugar and serve immediately. The pancake will fall on the way to the table, leaving a hollow for the toppings.

Rhode Island Jonnycakes

Never put an "h" in jonnycakes. The name derives, no doubt, from journey cakes, little corn cakes so called because they "traveled" so well. These corn-based griddle cakes have long been a staple in coastal New England, gaining fame in Rhode Island where there is a society dedicated to their preservation. Jonnycakes are firmer and drier than wheat flour pancakes and while they are served at breakfast alongside eggs and bacon, they are likely to turn up at any meal during the day, requiring, if anything, a pat of butter.

MAKES ABOUT 4 SERVINGS

> 1 cup stone-ground white cornmeal
> ¾ teaspoon salt
> ½ teaspoon sugar
> 1 to 1½ cups boiling water
> ¼ cup or more bacon fat or lard
> ¼ to ½ cup milk or light cream

1. In a heatproof bowl, combine the cornmeal, salt, and sugar. Stir in the boiling water, about ¼ cup at a time, until the mixture is thick and pasty. Let it stand until it "swells," 1 to 2 minutes.

2. While the mixture stands, heat the fat in a large cast-iron skillet over medium heat. Stir enough milk into the cornmeal mixture to make a batter that looks like slightly thin mashed potatoes. The batter should spread only slightly when dropped from a spoon.

3. Drop the batter by heaping serving-spoonfuls (about 2 tablespoons each) into the hot fat, pulling in the edges of the cakes with a metal spatula to prevent spreading. The cakes should be about ¼ inch thick or just thick enough to split.

4. Cook the cakes about 6 minutes per side, until they are golden brown and crusty. Adjust the heat to keep the cakes sizzling without browning too rapidly, and add more fat as needed. Drain the cakes on paper towels. Serve them hot, split, and with butter, if desired.

Kentucky Griddle Cakes

Early in the morning, mist drifts through the hollows of Kentucky's gentle hills. Then farmwives set the coffeepot on the back burner while they whip up a simple batter of cornmeal and buttermilk to make homey griddle cakes.

MAKES ABOUT 4 SERVINGS

> 1 cup yellow cornmeal
> ½ cup all-purpose flour
> 1 teaspoon sugar
> ¾ teaspoon salt
> ½ teaspoon baking powder
> ½ teaspoon baking soda
> 1 cup buttermilk
> 1 large egg
> 2 tablespoons vegetable oil
> 1 cup maple syrup, warmed

1. In a medium-size bowl, mix the cornmeal, flour, sugar, salt, baking powder, and baking soda. In a small bowl, combine the buttermilk, egg, and oil.

2. Stir the buttermilk mixture into the cornmeal mixture just until well blended. The batter will be slightly lumpy.

3. Lightly oil a griddle or a large skillet; heat over medium-high heat until a drop of water will dance across the surface. Stir the batter and drop a test cake on the griddle, using a scant ¼ cup batter.

4. Cook the pancake until bubbles burst on the top and the bottom is light brown. Turn and cook the other side 1 to 2 minutes, until it is browned. The light touch of a finger on the cake will leave no imprint. Add more buttermilk to the batter if the first cake does not spread well and adjust the heat if necessary. Serve the griddle cakes with warm syrup.

Dixieland Frycakes

Sweeten the batter with a couple of tablespoons of golden syrup (easy to find in the South), light molasses, or honey. Any one of them will give the frycakes pleasant sweetness and each one adds its own special flavor. Regular grits will bring texture to the cakes, and quick-cooking will give them smooth centers. Either way, the frycakes are crispy on the outside, creamy in the middle, and just fine with fresh fruit or homemade preserves.

MAKES ABOUT 4 SERVINGS

1½ cups boiling water
1⅓ cups regular or quick-cooking grits
2 tablespoons golden syrup, honey, or
  light molasses
1 tablespoon butter
¾ cup milk
⅔ cup all-purpose flour
4 teaspoons baking powder
¾ teaspoon salt
¼ cup vegetable oil
1 cup golden syrup, maple syrup, preserves,
  or fresh fruit

1. In a heatproof bowl, combine the boiling water and grits. Stir in 2 tablespoons syrup and the butter. Set aside 5 minutes.

2. Stir the milk into the grits mixture. In a sifter, combine the flour, baking powder, and salt. Sift the flour onto the grits mixture and stir until well combined.

3. In a large skillet, preferably with a non-stick surface, heat 1 teaspoon oil. Spoon the batter into the skillet to make several 3½-inch cakes. (The cakes are very fragile and will be difficult to turn if they are much larger.)

4. Fry the cakes until they are golden on one side. With a pancake turner, carefully turn the cakes and fry them until golden on the other side, adding more oil when necessary. Serve warm with syrup, preserves, or fresh fruit.

Three Grain Pancakes

(Photograph, Page 97)

Mixing cornmeal, which is a little gritty, in the batter gives these pancakes just a little crunch. Adding a measure of rye flour fills them with robust flavor. Warm syrup—maple or perhaps blueberry—makes them awfully good.

MAKES 4 SERVINGS

> 3 tablespoons butter or margarine
> 1¼ to 1½ cups milk
> 3 large eggs
> ¾ cup all-purpose flour
> ½ cup whole-wheat flour
> ½ cup rye flour
> ¼ cup stone-ground cornmeal
> 1½ tablespoons sugar
> 1 tablespoon baking powder
> 1 teaspoon salt
> ¼ teaspoon baking soda
> 1 cup maple syrup, warmed

1.   In a 1-quart saucepan over low heat, melt the butter; set aside to cool. In a small bowl, combine 1¼ cups milk and the eggs.

2.   In a medium-size bowl, mix the flours, cornmeal, sugar, baking powder, salt, and baking soda. Stir the milk mixture into the flour mixture just until well mixed. Stir in the melted butter. The batter should be slightly lumpy. Let the batter stand 20 to 30 minutes.

3.   Lightly oil a griddle or large skillet; heat over medium-high heat until a drop of water will dance across the surface. Stir the batter and drop a test cake on the griddle, using a scant ¼ cup batter.

4.   Cook the pancake until several bubbles burst on the top and the bottom is light brown. Turn and cook the other side 1 to 2 minutes, until it is browned. The light touch of a finger on the cake will leave no imprint. Add a bit more milk to the batter if the first cake does not spread well and adjust the heat if necessary. Serve the pancakes with warm syrup.

Basic Buttermilk Pancakes

Buttermilk pancakes, a little sweet, a little tangy, are an all-American breakfast. Stack a few on a farmhouse plate, spread a fair amount of creamy butter between them, and pour a liberal portion of pure maple syrup over the top. Now, that's breakfast!

MAKES ABOUT 4 SERVINGS

> ¼ cup (½ stick) butter or margarine
> 1⅓ cups buttermilk
> 1 large egg
> 1½ cups all-purpose flour
> 2 tablespoons sugar
> 1 teaspoon baking powder
> ¾ teaspoon baking soda
> ½ teaspoon salt
> 1 cup maple syrup, warmed

1.   In a 1-quart saucepan over low heat, melt the butter; set aside to cool. In a small bowl, combine the buttermilk and the egg.

2. In a medium-size bowl, mix the flour, sugar, baking powder, baking soda, and salt. Stir the buttermilk mixture into the flour mixture just until well combined. Stir in the melted butter. The batter should be lumpy.

3. Lightly oil a griddle or a large skillet; heat over medium-high heat until a drop of water will dance across the surface. Stir the batter and drop a test cake on the griddle, using a scant ¼ cup batter.

4. Cook the pancake until several bubbles burst on the top and the bottom is light brown. Turn and cook the other side 1 or 2 minutes, until it is browned. The light touch of a finger on the cake will leave no imprint. Add more buttermilk to the batter if the first cake does not spread well and adjust the heat if necessary. Serve the pancakes with warm syrup.

Cinnamon Pumpkin Pancakes

We continue to discover delicious new ways to cook with pumpkin, so good in so many country dishes. On an autumn morning when frost is in the air, mix up a batch of these spicy pumpkin pancakes. Serve them with marmalade or slices of fresh pineapple.

MAKES ABOUT 6 SERVINGS

> 2 cups all-purpose flour
> 2 tablespoons brown sugar
> 1 tablespoon baking powder
> 1 teaspoon salt
> 1 teaspoon ground cinnamon
> ¼ teaspoon ground nutmeg
> ¼ teaspoon ground ginger
> 1¾ cups milk
> ½ cup pumpkin puree (fresh or canned)
> 1 large egg
> 2 tablespoons vegetable oil
> 1½ cups maple syrup, warmed

1. In a medium-size bowl, mix the flour, sugar, baking powder, salt, and spices. In a small bowl, combine the milk, pumpkin, egg, and oil. Stir the milk mixture into the flour mixture just until well blended. The batter should be slightly lumpy.

2. Lightly oil a griddle or a large skillet; heat over medium-high heat until a drop of water will dance across the surface.

3. Spoon about ¼ cup batter onto the griddle for each pancake. Cook until several bubbles burst on the top and the bottom is light brown. Turn and cook the other side about 2 minutes, until it is browned. The light touch of a finger on the cake will leave no imprint. Add more milk to the batter if the first cake does not spread well and adjust the heat if necessary. Serve the pancakes with warm syrup.

Raspberry Sourdough Griddle Cakes

Sourdough griddle cakes have a distinctive tang achieved no other way except by using a sourdough starter for the batter. These tender griddle cakes also taste good with salmonberries. These wild raspberries are grown in the northwestern U.S., and take their name from the warm red color they have when fully ripe.

MAKES ABOUT 4 SERVINGS

SOURDOUGH STARTER:
2 cups warm water (105° to 115°F)
1 package active dry yeast
2½ cups whole-wheat flour

1½ cups all-purpose flour
2 tablespoons sugar
1 teaspoon salt
½ teaspoon ground allspice
¼ teaspoon baking soda
1 cup milk
1 large egg
2 tablespoons vegetable oil
1½ cups raspberries or salmonberries
1 cup golden or maple syrup, warmed

1. Several hours or one day before making the griddle cakes, prepare the Sourdough Starter: In a medium-size bowl or 1½-quart container, combine the water, yeast, and flour. Let stand at least 2 hours but preferably overnight. Then cover and refrigerate the starter until you are ready to use it. When some of the starter is used, replace it with ½ cup flour, ½ cup warm water, and 1 teaspoon sugar for each cup removed.

2. In a large bowl, mix the all-purpose flour, sugar, salt, allspice, and baking soda. In a small bowl, combine the milk, egg, and oil. Stir the milk mixture and 1 cup sourdough starter into the flour mixture just until well mixed. Gently fold in the berries.

3. Lightly oil a griddle or a large skillet; heat over medium-high heat until a drop of water will dance across the surface.

4. Spoon about ⅓ cup batter onto the griddle for each griddle cake. Cook until several bubbles burst on the top and the bottom is golden brown. Turn and cook the other side 1 to 2 minutes, until it is browned. The light touch of a finger on the cake will leave no imprint. Add more milk to the batter if the first cake does not spread well and adjust the heat if necessary. Serve the griddle cakes with warm syrup.

Raisin Cornmeal Pancakes

We all know that fresh, fiber-rich foods are essential to a healthy eating program. One good (and tasty) source of fiber is a serving of these whole-wheat and cornmeal pancakes dotted with raisins.

MAKES ABOUT 6 SERVINGS

3 large eggs
2½ cups whole-wheat flour
1 cup yellow cornmeal
1 tablespoon baking powder
1 teaspoon salt
2 cups milk
¾ cup vegetable oil
1 teaspoon honey
1 cup dark seedless raisins
1½ cups maple syrup, warmed

1. Separate the eggs, placing the whites in a medium-size bowl and the yolks in a small bowl. Let them warm to room temperature.

2. In a large bowl, mix the flour, cornmeal, baking powder, and salt. Stir the milk, oil, and honey into the yolks. Stir the milk mixture into the flour mixture just until well blended. The batter will be slightly lumpy. Add the raisins and stir to mix well.

3. With an electric mixer on high speed, beat the whites until stiff peaks form. Fold the whites into the batter until no streaks of white remain.

4. Lightly oil a griddle or a large skillet; heat over medium-high heat until a drop of water will dance across the surface. Drop a test cake on the griddle, using a scant ⅓ cup batter.

5. Cook the pancake until bubbles burst on the top and the bottom is light brown. Turn and cook the other side 1 to 2 minutes, until it is browned. The light touch of a finger on the cake will leave no imprint. Add a bit more milk to the batter if the first cake does not spread well and adjust the heat if necessary. Serve the pancakes with warm syrup.

Blueberry Griddle Cakes

Hearty, low-growing blueberry bushes tenaciously hug the windy, rock-bound coast of Maine, producing what are thought to be the best blueberries in the world. Every year, Nor'easterners gather the tiny berries, so full of sweet good flavor, often searching out the wild bushes early in the day before the fog has rolled off the sea. Then they toss a heaping handful into the batter for morning griddle cakes.

MAKES ABOUT 3 SERVINGS

1¼ cups all-purpose flour
1 tablespoon sugar
1 tablespoon baking powder
¼ teaspoon salt
1¼ cups milk
1 large egg
1 tablespoon vegetable oil
½ cup blueberries
1 cup blueberry or other syrup, warmed

1. In a medium-size bowl, mix the flour, sugar, baking powder, and salt. In a small bowl, combine the milk, egg, and oil. Stir the milk mixture into the flour mixture just until well mixed. The batter will be slightly lumpy. Fold the blueberries into the batter.

2. Lightly oil a griddle or a large skillet; heat over medium-high heat until a drop of water will dance across the surface.

3. Spoon about ⅓ cup batter onto the griddle for each pancake. Cook until several bubbles burst on the top and the bottom is light brown. Turn and cook the other side about 2 minutes, until it is browned. The light touch of a finger on the cake will leave no imprint. Add more milk to the batter if the first cake does not spread well and adjust the heat if necessary. Serve the griddle cakes with warm syrup.

Classic Waffles

"Quintessential" might be a good description of our classic waffles. These are the most versatile ones we've found, working equally well with light or hearty, sweet or savory toppings. Do try them!

MAKES 6 SERVINGS

> ¼ cup (½ stick) butter or margarine
> 1½ cups all-purpose flour
> 1 tablespoon sugar
> 2 teaspoons baking powder
> ½ teaspoon salt
> 1½ cups milk
> 3 large eggs, separated, at room
>   temperature

1.   Heat the waffle iron. In a 1-quart saucepan, melt the butter over low heat. Set aside to cool slightly.

2.   In a large bowl, combine the flour, sugar, baking powder, and salt.

3.   Beat the milk, then the egg yolks into the melted butter. Stir this into the flour mixture just until moistened.

4.   In a small bowl, with an electric mixer on high speed, beat the egg whites until stiff peaks form. Fold the whites into the waffle batter just until blended.

5.   Ladle or pour enough batter over the hot waffle iron to cover two-thirds of the grid. With a metal spatula, spread the batter to the edges of the grid. Close the lid and cook the waffle until the steam stops, about 5 minutes. When the waffle is done, lift the lid and remove it with a fork. Continue with the remaining batter.

The Waffle Iron

Just as waffles evolved from sacramental wafers, so has the waffle maker undergone its share of changes. The electrified versions of today take most of the work and perhaps much of the challenge in making crisp old-fashioned waffles.

Wafer irons were used in Europe during the 12th century to shape and bake batter into thin decorative wafers which were served on religious feast days. Similar irons were produced later to bake crisp thin cookies. The Pilgrims enjoyed waffles made on a simple-gridded iron imported from Holland. Thomas Jefferson fancied a long-handled French version which made *gaufres,* or thin wafers.

During the 19th century, cooks baked sweet waffle batter in long-handled irons held over an open-hearth fire. Later, they used stovetop cast-iron waffle makers that they flipped over during cooking for even baking. (If you are lucky, you may find an old waffle maker or even a long-handled cookie iron at a flea market or an antiques shop.)

By the 1930s, electric waffle irons simplified waffle-making. Nowadays, you can find deep-gridded Belgian waffle irons and heart-shaped waffle irons, common are round, square, and rectangular waffle makers. Some have been so well designed that you can make waffles right at the table. Though the technology and even the shape of the waffle iron has changed through the centuries, folks everywhere will always find it hard to turn down a sweet, golden waffle.

Hash Brown Potatoes, recipe page 123
Scrambled Eggs, recipe page 88

Farmstead Waffles

Creamy, farm-fresh buttermilk, eggs, and butter work together in these old-fashioned waffles. The best way to eat them is with golden clover honey, warmed in a small pan just until it is easy to pour.

MAKES 6 SERVINGS

> ¼ cup (½ stick) butter or margarine
> 2 cups all-purpose flour
> 2 teaspoons baking powder
> 1 teaspoon baking soda
> ½ teaspoon salt
> 2 cups buttermilk
> 3 large eggs

1.   Heat the waffle iron. In a 1-quart saucepan, melt the butter over low heat. Set aside to cool slightly.

2.   In a large bowl, combine the flour, baking powder, baking soda, and salt.

3.   Beat the buttermilk, then the eggs into the melted butter. Stir this into the flour mixture just until moistened.

4.   Ladle or pour enough batter over the hot waffle iron to cover two-thirds of the grid. With a metal spatula, spread the batter to the edges of the grid. Close the lid and cook the waffle until the steam stops, about 5 minutes. When the waffle is done, lift the lid and remove it with a fork. Continue with the remaining batter.

Homemade Muesli, recipe page 114
Crunchy Almond Granola, recipe page 114
Apple and Pineapple Muesli, recipe page 115

Cocoa-Nut Waffles

There is a gentle sweetness in these cocoa-nut waffles. Try them with fresh raspberries and cream or, for a heartier meal, some thick homemade applesauce and raisins.

MAKES 6 SERVINGS

> ½ cup (1 stick) butter or margarine
> 1½ cups sifted cake flour
> ¾ cup sugar
> ¼ cup unsweetened cocoa powder
> 1 teaspoon baking powder
> ½ teaspoon baking soda
> ¼ teaspoon salt
> 1½ cups buttermilk
> 2 large eggs
> 1 teaspoon vanilla extract
> ½ cup finely chopped walnuts

1.   Heat the waffle iron. In a 1-quart saucepan, melt the butter over low heat. Set aside to cool slightly.

2.   Into a medium-size bowl, sift together the flour, sugar, cocoa, baking powder, baking soda, and salt.

3.   Beat the buttermilk, then the eggs and the vanilla into the melted butter. Stir this into the flour mixture just until moistened. Fold in the nuts.

4.   Ladle or pour enough batter over the hot waffle iron to cover two-thirds of the grid. With a metal spatula, spread the batter to the edges of the grid. Close the lid and cook until the steam stops, about 5 minutes. When the waffle is done, lift the lid and remove it with a fork. Continue with the remaining batter.

Herb and Onion Waffles

For those who prefer savory waffles to sweet, herbed waffles are a delicious answer. The waffle batter is perfumed with the heady scents of parsley, sage, and thyme, and a judicious grating of onion, then lightened with clouds of fluffy egg white. The golden waffles can be served with Crème Fraîche (page 84), creamed chicken, or fresh butter.

MAKES 6 SERVINGS

> 6 tablespoons butter or margarine
> 2 cups all-purpose flour
> 1 tablespoon baking powder
> ½ teaspoon salt
> 1¾ cups milk
> 2 large eggs, separated, at room temperature
> 1 tablespoon chopped fresh parsley leaves
> 1 tablespoon grated onion
> ½ teaspoon dried rubbed sage
> ½ teaspoon dried thyme leaves

1.   Heat the waffle iron. In a 1-quart saucepan, melt the butter over low heat. Set aside to cool slightly.

2.   In a medium-size bowl, combine the flour, baking powder, and salt. Set aside.

3.   Beat the milk, then the egg yolks, parsley, onion, sage, and thyme into the melted butter. Stir this into the flour mixture just until moistened.

4.   In a small bowl, with an electric mixer, beat the egg whites until stiff peaks form. Fold the whites into the waffle batter.

5.   Ladle or pour enough batter over the hot waffle iron to cover two-thirds of the grid. With a metal spatula, spread the batter to the edges of the grid. Close the lid and cook until the steam stops, about 5 minutes. When the waffle is done, lift the lid and remove it with a fork. Continue with the remaining batter.

Honey Whole-wheat Waffles

An equal measure of whole-wheat and all-purpose flours lends these honey-sweet waffles sturdy texture and mellow flavor. For a warming, filling breakfast on a snowy day, try them with our tart Cranberries in Syrup (page 85).

MAKES 8 SERVINGS

> ¼ cup (½ stick) butter or margarine
> 1 cup all-purpose flour
> 1 cup whole-wheat flour
> 2 teaspoons baking powder
> 2 teaspoons sugar
> ½ teaspoon salt
> 2 cups milk
> ¼ cup honey
> 3 large eggs, separated, at room temperature

1. Heat the waffle iron. In a 1-quart saucepan, melt the butter over low heat. Set aside to cool slightly.

2. In a medium-size bowl, combine both flours, the baking powder, sugar, and salt.

3. Beat the milk and honey, then the egg yolks, into the melted butter. Stir this into the flour mixture just until moistened.

4. In a small bowl, with an electric mixer, beat the egg whites until stiff peaks form. Fold the whites into the waffle batter just until blended.

5. Ladle or pour enough batter over the hot waffle iron to cover two-thirds of the grid. With a metal spatula, spread the batter to the edges of the grid. Close the lid and cook until the steam stops, about 5 minutes. When the waffle is done, lift the lid and remove it with a fork. Continue with the remaining batter.

Buckwheat Waffles

Buckwheat grows in the cooler regions of the country such as northern, inland Maine and upstate New York. There, a platter stacked with just-cooked waffles sweetened with Mulled Cider Syrup (page 85) is a pretty sight on a chilly morning.

MAKES 6 SERVINGS

1½ cups milk
2 tablespoons molasses
2 tablespoons butter or margarine
1 package active dry yeast
½ cup warm water (105° to 115°F)
1 large egg
1 cup all-purpose flour
½ cup buckwheat flour
½ teaspoon salt

1. In a 1-quart saucepan, heat the milk just until bubbles form around the side of the pan. Remove the milk from the heat and stir in the molasses and butter. Cool the mixture to warm. In a medium-size bowl, sprinkle the yeast over the water; stir and set aside to soften, about 5 minutes.

2. Beat the egg into the yeast mixture. Add the flours and salt alternately with the warm milk mixture, stirring with a wire whisk until well blended. Cover the batter with a cloth and let it rise in a warm place, away from drafts, until it is double in size, about 45 minutes.

3. Heat the waffle iron. Stir down the waffle batter.

4. Ladle or pour enough batter over the hot waffle iron to cover two-thirds of the grid. With a metal spatula, spread the batter to the edges of the grid. Close the lid and cook until the steam stops, about 5 minutes. When the waffle is done, lift the lid and remove it with a fork. Continue with the remaining batter.

Pomegranate Sauce

Pomegranate seeds are tiny, ruby-red globes bursting with a tart but never bitter juice. They taste of autumn, when the fruit is in season. Use the juice to make this delicate, bright red sauce, so good poured over pancakes or waffles and so pretty served in a small cut-glass pitcher or bowl.

MAKES 2⅓ CUPS

> 2 cups pomegranate juice (about 4 pomegranates)
> ¾ cup sugar
> 2 tablespoons cornstarch
> 1 tablespoon lime juice
> 1 tablespoon butter

1. To release the seeds from pomegranates for making juice, with the tip of a knife, score the fruit's leathery skin into 6 or 8 equal wedges. Separate the pomegranate into wedge-shaped sections. Pomegranate seeds will stain fingers so you may want to wear gloves. To keep the seeds from splattering, submerge the fruit sections in a bowl of cold water as you work with them. With your fingers, gently remove the seeds from the skin and its papery membrane. The seeds will sink and the membrane will float. Discard the skin and the membrane. Strain the seeds from the water.

2. To extract the juice, place the seeds, 2 cups at a time, in an electric blender or food processor. Using an on-and-off motion, blend just until the seeds are crushed. Do not overblend or you will be grinding the seeds. Strain the juice through a strainer lined with dampened cheesecloth.

3. In a 1-quart saucepan, combine the sugar and the cornstarch. Stir in the pomegranate juice. Heat to boiling over medium-high heat, stirring constantly. Boil 1 minute, until the mixture is thickened and clear.

4. Remove the sauce from the heat. Stir in the lime juice and the butter. Serve warm.

Crème Fraîche

You can buy sinfully rich, smooth crème fraîche in specialty stores, or, with a little planning, make your own. Thick, creamy, and just a bit tart, the flavor is richer than that of whipped cream. Try it spooned over freshly cut peaches, plums, and sun-ripe berries heaped on a hot waffle.

MAKES ABOUT 1½ CUPS

> 1 cup (½ pint) heavy cream
> ½ cup sour cream

In a bowl, combine the creams; cover the bowl with plastic wrap. Let the cream stand at room temperature until it has thickened, 16 to 24 hours. Before serving, refrigerate the cream until it is cold. Crème fraîche will keep up to a week.

Cranberries in Syrup

Spoon this whole-berry syrup over waffles and pancakes, or whip it into softened butter for an extra-rich breakfast spread; see the recipe for Cranberry Butter on page (178).

MAKES ABOUT 2½ CUPS

> 1 cup water
> ½ cup sugar
> ½ 12-ounce package cranberries
> ¼ cup maple syrup
> ¼ cup coarsely chopped pecans
> 1 teaspoon grated lemon rind

1. In a 2-quart saucepan, combine the water and sugar. Cook, without stirring, over medium heat until the sugar dissolves.

2. Stir in the cranberries, maple syrup, nuts, and lemon rind. Simmer just until the berries begin to pop, about 5 minutes. Remove from the heat.

3. Serve cranberries warm or cover and store in the refrigerator until ready to use.

Mulled Cider Syrup

The mellow flavors of autumn—freshly pressed apple cider, cinnamon, cloves, and nutmeg—team up to make a spicy syrup for any variety of waffles or pancakes.

MAKES 2½ CUPS

> 2 cups apple cider
> ¼ cup granulated sugar
> ¼ cup firmly packed light-brown sugar
> ½ cup apple jelly
> ½ teaspoon ground cinnamon
> ¼ teaspoon ground cloves
> ¼ teaspoon ground nutmeg

1. In a 1-quart saucepan, combine the cider and sugars. Cook, without stirring, over medium heat until the sugars dissolve.

2. Stir in the jelly, cinnamon, cloves, and nutmeg. Heat to boiling. Reduce heat to low and simmer, stirring, until the jelly melts. Serve warm.

Eggs

Stop a moment and consider the egg sitting in your hand. If you are lucky, the one you are holding is still warm from its nesting place under the hen. A gentle prod and the silly bird, with no more protesting than a quick ruffle of her feathers and a dull cluck, hopped off her roosting place and let you gather the perfect egg she produced in the night. No egg will ever taste better.

Most of us, however, hold a storebought egg in our hand. Still a miraculous thing, which we depend on in so many ways. As important as eggs are in baking, dessert, and sauce making for leavening, lightening, binding, and thickening, nowhere are they better showcased than on the morning table. At this time of day, we like them cooked nearly any way. We prefer them fresh—eggs packed in their cartons will keep in the refrigerator for up to a month but they are tastiest when fresh.

These days, a number of supermarkets, specialty stores, natural food stores, and greengrocers are selling eggs labeled "country", "organic" or "free-range." Buy these if you can. They are, most likely, from a local farm where the laying hens are allowed to wander freely in a pen or large coop. The eggs will cost a little more, but unless you have your own chicken coop, they are the freshest available. Country eggs may be white or brown, it makes no difference. The flavor is the same. The color merely signifies whether a white- or red-earlobed hen laid the egg.

Beginning with the freshest eggs is just the beginning. Cooking eggs correctly is crucial. They must be cooked over medium or low heat for the least possible amount of time. Overcooking is the greatest injustice that can be done to eggs. When exposed to heat that is too high, or when cooked too long, the protein in the egg whites toughens and turns rubbery. Here we explain how to cook the perfect fried, scrambled, poached, baked or in-the-shell egg.

Basic Eggs

Fried

In a skillet, melt 1 tablespoon butter, margarine, or bacon fat over medium heat until it sizzles. Crack the egg into a saucer and gently slide it into the skillet. Immediately reduce the heat and cook the egg slowly to desired doneness. To cook the top, spoon some melted butter over it or flip it over. Or, add 1 teaspoon water, cover tightly, remove from the heat, and check after 1 minute.

Scrambled

(Photograph, page 79)

In a bowl, beat the eggs with milk or water (1 tablespoon per egg) and a pinch of salt, pepper, or herbs (dill, chervil, and basil are good). In a skillet, melt 1 tablespoon butter or margarine over medium heat until it sizzles. (Increase the amount for more than 4 eggs.) Reduce the heat to medium-low, and pour the eggs into the skillet. Cook them until the mixture begins to set on the bottom. Draw a pancake turner across the bottom of the skillet, forming large, soft curds of egg. Continue until the eggs are thickened but still moist. Remove them from the pan immediately. Eggs will continue to cook after they are removed from the pan, and would be overcooked if they remained over the heat until firm.

Poached

If you are using a poacher, generously butter the cups. Heat water to boiling; add the eggs, cover, and simmer 3 minutes. To poach eggs in a skillet, lightly oil the skillet. Add enough water to make 1 inch in the pan and 2 tablespoons white vinegar (which will help the whites set). Heat to boiling. Adjust the heat until the water is just simmering. Crack the eggs, 1 at a time, onto a saucer and gently slip them into the simmering water. Do not overcrowd the eggs; they should not touch. After 2½ minutes, the whites will be firm but the yolks will remain runny and soft. Simmer 3 to 5 minutes, depending upon desired doneness. Lift the eggs from the water with a slotted spoon or pancake turner. Drain them well on paper towels and trim away any ragged edges.

Baked

Heat the oven to 325°F. Grease individual ramekins or custard cups, or a shallow 8-inch baking dish. Break 1 or 2 eggs into each ramekin, or as many as 12 into the baking dish. For each egg, add 1 tablespoon milk, cream, broth, or seasoned tomato sauce. Season lightly with freshly ground pepper or herbs. Bake the eggs 12 to 20 minutes depending upon desired doneness and the number of eggs in dish—12 minutes for 1 egg in a custard cup to 20 minutes for 12 eggs in baking dish.

In-the-Shell

Put the eggs in a saucepan, being careful not to overcrowd them. Add cold water to an inch above the eggs. Heat the water to boiling. Remove the pan from the heat; cover and set aside. For soft-cooked eggs, let the eggs stand 2 to 4 minutes (depending on how well-done you like them) and 15 minutes for hard-cooked eggs. The cooking times are for large size eggs. When the eggs are ready, cool them quickly under cold water.

Herb Flower Omelet

When the aromatic plants in your herb garden start to flower, snip their blooms and stir them into eggs and cheese for a pungent omelet.

MAKES 1 SERVING

2 large eggs
2 tablespoons water
Pinch of salt
Pinch of ground black pepper
1 tablespoon butter or margarine
3 tablespoons shredded Cheddar cheese
2 tablespoons chopped herb flowers (from chives, parsley, chervil, or basil)

1. In a small bowl, combine the eggs, water, salt, and pepper until well blended.

2. In a small omelet pan or skillet, melt the butter over medium heat, tilting the skillet to grease the bottom and side of the pan. Pour in the egg mixture. As the mixture begins to set, lift the edge of eggs all the way around the side of the pan to allow the uncooked portion to flow to the bottom.

3. Sprinkle the omelet with the cheese and herb flowers. Tilt the pan and slide the omelet to the edge. Fold or roll the omelet and invert it onto a plate. Garnish with fresh herb flowers, if desired.

Scrambled Eggs Deluxe

Your scrambled eggs will get high remarks for composition (thanks to the addition of caviar) and presentation (by virtue of spooning them back into their shells). For more drama, choose eggs with brown shells.

MAKES 2 SERVINGS

4 large eggs
1 tablespoon water
⅛ teaspoon ground white pepper
1 tablespoon butter
2 teaspoons red-salmon or golden caviar

1. Into a medium-size bowl, crack and open each egg at the broad end, keeping the rest of the shell intact. Rinse the shells, drain, and set them upright in 4 egg cups. Add the water and pepper to the eggs and beat until they are well mixed.

2. In a skillet, melt the butter over medium heat until it begins to sizzle. Pour the egg mixture into skillet and cook until it begins to set on the bottom. Draw the tip of a pancake turner across the bottom of the skillet, forming large, soft curds of egg. Continue to cook just until eggs are thickened but still moist. Remove them from heat.

3. With a teaspoon, spoon the scrambled eggs into each shell. Top with caviar.

Ramp-and-Potato Egg Scramble

(Photograph, page 98)

Wild onions with the flavor of garlic and leeks, ramps are showing up more and more often in farmers' markets and greengrocers. (In West Virginia, locals celebrate this neglected vegetable with their annual Ramp Festival.) Ramps blend nicely with freshly dug red potatoes and eggs, requiring no more seasoning than a few turns of the pepper mill. Leeks can be substituted for the ramps, but include only the white part, and sauté them with the potatoes.

MAKES 6 SERVINGS

> 6 small (about ¾ pound) red potatoes
> 6 large eggs
> ⅓ cup water
> ¼ teaspoon salt
> ⅛ teaspoon ground black pepper
> 2 tablespoons butter or margarine
> ½ cup chopped ramps (white bulbs and
>   green tops)

1. In a steamer or a 4-quart saucepan with a wire rack, steam the potatoes over boiling water until just tender, about 30 minutes. Drain and cool the potatoes until they are easy to handle. Cut the potatoes into ¾-inch chunks.

2. In a small bowl, beat the eggs, water, salt, and pepper until blended.

3. In a 10-inch skillet, melt the butter over medium heat. Add the potatoes. Cook 3 to 5 minutes, until lightly browned, turning the potatoes occasionally with a pancake turner. Add the ramps and cook a few seconds longer.

4. Pour the egg mixture into the skillet. Stir from the edge toward the center of the skillet until the eggs begin to set. Cover and cook a few minutes longer, until the eggs are just set.

Puffy Omelet

Mastering the art of the omelet is a mark of a good cook. In our recipe, we've added cream of tartar and cornstarch to stabilize the temperamental eggs, and lightly seasoned the omelet with salt and pepper. The result is an omelet that is delicate, airy, and pale as butter.

MAKES 6 SERVINGS

> 8 large eggs
> ½ teaspoon cream of tartar
> 2 tablespoons all-purpose flour
> 1 tablespoon cornstarch
> ½ teaspoon salt
> ⅛ teaspoon ground black pepper
> 1 tablespoon butter or margarine

1. Heat the oven to 350°F. Separate the eggs, placing the whites in a large bowl and the yolks in a small bowl. Let them warm to room temperature. With an electric mixer at high speed, beat the whites and the cream of tartar until stiff peaks form. With the same beaters, beat together the yolks, flour, cornstarch, salt, and pepper until smooth.

2. In a heavy 10-inch skillet with an oven-safe handle, melt the butter, tilting the skillet to grease the bottom and side of the pan. Fold the yolk mixture into the whites. Spoon the mixture into the skillet.

3. Bake the omelet 25 to 30 minutes, or until the top is golden brown and the center seems firm when the skillet is gently tapped. Serve immediately.

Summertime Corn Souffle

Here's a good recipe for late summer, when the corn is as high as an elephant's eye. Kernels cut from fresh cooked ears (please, no canned or frozen corn) are folded into the souffle batter, which gets its lively, spicy bite from chilies or peppers, green onions, and a hot red-pepper sauce such as Tabasco.

MAKES 6 SERVINGS

> **6 large eggs**
> **1 cup water**
> **½ cup quick-cooking grits**
> **1 cup milk**
> **½ teaspoon salt**
> **2 tablespoons butter or margarine**
> **¼ cup diced fresh green chilies or sweet green pepper**
> **¼ cup chopped green onions**
> **1½ cups shredded sharp Cheddar cheese**
> **1½ cups cooked whole-kernel corn**
> **Dash to a few drops hot red-pepper sauce**
> **⅛ teaspoon ground nutmeg**

1. Separate the eggs, placing the whites in the large bowl of an electric mixer and the yolks in a cup. Let them warm to room temperature. Butter a 2-quart souffle dish and set aside.

2. In a heavy 2-quart saucepan, heat the water to boiling over high heat. In a small bowl, combine the grits, milk, and salt. Stir the grits mixture into the boiling water. Cook, stirring constantly, until the mixture is thickened and bubbly, about 5 minutes. Cover and cook over low heat 5 minutes.

3. Meanwhile, in a small skillet, melt the butter over medium heat. Add the chilies and green onions; sauté 1 minute. Remove from the heat. Stir the chilies, onions, cheese, corn, red-pepper sauce, and nutmeg into the grits, then remove from the heat. Stir the yolks into the grits mixture until well combined. Set aside to cool slightly.

4. Heat the oven to 400°F. With the mixer at high speed, beat the whites until stiff, but not dry, peaks form. Gently fold the whites into the grits mixture until no white streaks remain. Quickly spoon the batter into the buttered dish.

5. Bake the souffle 35 to 45 minutes, or until it is puffy and golden brown. The center will appear set when the dish is gently tapped. Serve the souffle immediately.

The Goodness of Eggs

With only 80 calories per large egg, eggs are a very good source of high-quality protein. They contain all the necessary vitamins except Vitamin C, and many important minerals. Each large egg contains about 260 mg. of cholesterol.

Creamy Eggs and Grits

A panful of eggs cooked up with grits makes a hearty meal on a cold, blustery morning. Since the grits must be cooked ahead of time and then set in the refrigerator overnight, this is an easy breakfast to make even when it is *very* early in the morning.

MAKES 6 SERVINGS

> 3 cups water
> ¾ cup quick-cooking grits
> ¾ teaspoon salt
> 8 large eggs
> 2 tablespoons milk
> 2 tablespoons finely chopped green onion
> ⅛ teaspoon ground black pepper
> 1 tablespoon butter or margarine
> 1 3-ounce package cream cheese, cut into
> ½-inch cubes

1. Several hours or the night before serving, prepare the grits: In a heavy 2-quart saucepan, heat 2¼ cups water to boiling over high heat. In a small bowl, combine the grits, ½ teaspoon salt, and ¾ cup water. Stir the grits mixture into the boiling water. Cook, stirring constantly, until the mixture is thickened and bubbly, about 5 minutes. Cover and cook over low heat 5 minutes.

2. Generously grease an 8-inch-square baking pan. Pour the grits into the greased pan and cool to room temperature. Tightly cover the pan and refrigerate until the grits are firm, several hours or overnight.

3. About 15 minutes before serving, cut the grits into ½-inch squares. In a medium-size bowl, beat the eggs with a fork until they are frothy. Stir in the milk, green onion, pepper, and remaining ¼ teaspoon salt.

4. In a large skillet, melt the butter over medium heat. Add the grits and sauté, stirring gently, until they are golden brown on the edges. Add the egg mixture and cream cheese. As the eggs begin to set, lift the edge of eggs all the way around the side of the pan to allow the uncooked portion to flow to the bottom. Cook until the eggs are just set.

A Bit About Grits

Mild-flavored and porridge-like, grits are comforting food, indeed. Southern cooks have relied on them for generations—alongside country ham or in spoon bread. The word itself comes from the Old English *grytt,* meaning bran.

At one time, grits were actually coarsely ground hominy. Hominy is made by soaking white or yellow corn kernels in a water-lye solution to remove the hulls (outer coating). This treatment in turn puffs up the soft inner portion of the kernels; then the corn kernels are dried. If they're cracked, they'll form grits. However, most are cooked, canned, and sold as puffy kernels of hominy.

Today's hominy grits are made in the same process which produces cornmeal and corn flour. The kernels of the corn are steamed, rather than lye-treated, to loosen the hulls. Once the corn is hulled, dried, and cracked, the largest granules are grits, the medium-size ones are cornmeal, and the finest particles become corn flour. In the market, you'll find regular grits which are large granules and require longer cooking than either quick grits which are small granules, or dried, precooked instant grits.

Baked Ham Strata

For a substantial, tasty breakfast, set a pitcher of fresh juice and a basket of simple muffins out with this egg-based casserole. Layered with buttered cubes of toast and generous quantities of ham and mild Swiss cheese, the dish must be prepared ahead of time, making it ideal for weekends when you have a houseful of guests.

MAKES 8 SERVINGS

> 12 slices firm white bread
> 3 tablespoons butter or margarine, softened
> 2½ cups milk
> 5 large eggs
> 4 teaspoons Dijon-style prepared mustard
> ¼ teaspoon salt
> ¼ teaspoon ground black pepper
> ¾ pound Swiss or Jarlsberg cheese, shredded
> ½ pound baked or boiled ham, diced
> 3 green onions, trimmed and sliced or chopped
> Green onion curls (optional)

1. Toast the bread and spread one side of each with butter. Cut the toast into ¾-inch pieces.

2. In a bowl, whisk together the milk, eggs, mustard, salt, and pepper. Butter a 13- by 9-inch baking dish. Place half the toast pieces in the dish. Sprinkle these with half the cheese, ham, and sliced onions. Repeat layering with the other half of the ingredients.

3. Slowly pour the egg mixture over the casserole to moisten the toast. Cover the dish with aluminum foil. Refrigerate at least 2 hours or overnight.

4. Before serving, heat the oven to 350°F. Bake the strata 45 minutes. Remove the foil and bake 5 to 10 minutes longer, or until the top is lightly browned. Let the strata stand 5 minutes before serving. If desired, garnish it with green onion curls: Trim the root ends from the onion and cut it into 3-inch lengths. With a small, sharp knife, make crisscross cuts about 1-inch deep at both ends of each onion piece. Place them in a bowl of ice water, cover, and refrigerate until the ends curl.

Storing Eggs

Fresh eggs may be stored in their carton in the refrigerator for as long as a month. Eggs are porous so keep them covered and away from foods with strong odors. Leftover raw egg whites may be kept tightly covered in a jar and refrigerated up to a week. Egg yolks are fragile and difficult to store. Unbroken yolks should be covered with a bit of water and used within two days. Raw whole eggs, whites, and yolks may be frozen, out of the shell, in tightly covered freezer containers. (To prevent thickening, add ⅛ teaspoon salt or 1½ teaspoons sugar or light corn syrup for every four yolks or two whole eggs.) It's a good idea to label the container with the number of eggs and any ingredient added. Salted eggs are meant for main dishes and sweetened ones for desserts. Thaw frozen eggs overnight in the refrigerator and use them as soon as they are thawed. Hard-cooked eggs should be refrigerated as soon as they are cooled and will keep four or five days.

Spinach and Cheddar Cheese Souffle

A golden, puffy souffle will elevate the most mundane morning. The secret to a good souffle is to work quickly and steadily without panicking. Separate the eggs while they are cold (it's easier) but let the whites warm to room temperature before beating them. Once the souffle is in the oven, watch the time carefully and take it out not a minute too late, or it may collapse. But remember, a fallen souffle tastes mighty good, too.

MAKES 6 SERVINGS

> 6 large eggs
> 2 teaspoons butter or margarine
> ⅓ cup all-purpose flour
> ½ teaspoon salt
> 1¼ cups milk
> ½ cup shredded Cheddar cheese
> ½ 10-ounce package frozen chopped
>   spinach, thawed
> ¼ teaspoon dried basil
> ¼ teaspoon cream of tartar

1. Separate the eggs, placing the whites in the large bowl of an electric mixer and the yolks in a medium-size bowl. Let them warm to room temperature.

2. Cut a piece of waxed paper 27 inches long and fold it lengthwise in thirds. Butter one side of the folded waxed-paper strip with some softened butter. Place the strip, buttered-side in, around the outside of a 2-quart souffle dish so that at least 2 inches extend above the top of the dish. To hold it in place, tie the waxed paper tightly with string just below the rim of the dish. Spread the remaining butter over the side and bottom of the souffle dish.

3. In a 2-quart saucepan, combine the flour and salt. Gradually add half the milk, beating until the mixture is smooth. Scrape the side and bottom of the pan with a rubber spatula. Add the remaining milk, beating until there are no lumps.

4. Heat the milk mixture to boiling over medium heat, stirring constantly. Cook, continuing to stir constantly, until the mixture is thick. Remove from the heat.

5. Heat the oven to 350°F. Beat the yolks with a wire whisk. Gradually beat in the thickened milk mixture. Return half the mixture to the saucepan.

6. Fold the cheese into the sauce in the saucepan. Drain the spinach well and squeeze dry. Fold the spinach and the basil into the sauce in the bowl.

7. Add the cream of tartar to the egg whites. With the electric mixer at medium-high speed, beat the whites until stiff, but not dry, peaks form.

8. Gently fold half the whites into the cheese mixture and half into the spinach mixture, until no white streaks remain. Spoon the cheese mixture into the prepared souffle dish, pushing it toward the side. Spoon the spinach mixture into the center.

9. Bake 35 to 40 minutes, or until the souffle is puffed and golden brown, and the center appears set when the dish is gently tapped. Carefully remove the waxed-paper strip and serve the souffle immediately.

Manor House Eggs

For those who love fancy breakfast dishes, we've developed what may be the ultimate shrimp and egg recipe. Fresh spinach, Parmesan cheese, and Dijon mustard contribute color and flavor to Manor House Eggs. If you prefer, you can use shrimps with the heads still attached; in this case, allow one full pound.

MAKES 4 SERVINGS

> 6 large eggs
> ¾ pound medium-size shrimp
> 2 tablespoons butter
> 1½ tablespoons all-purpose flour
> 1⅓ cups milk
> 2 tablespoons grated Parmesan cheese
> 1 teaspoon lemon juice
> 1 teaspoon Dijon-style prepared mustard
> 2 pounds fresh spinach
> Salt and ground black pepper to taste

1. In a 2-quart saucepan, place the eggs and enough cold water to cover 1 inch above the eggs. Heat the eggs over high heat just until the water comes to a full boil. Cover the pan and remove from the heat. Let the eggs stand 10 minutes. Pour off the water and cool the eggs under running cold water.

2. Shell and devein most of the shrimp, setting aside a few with shells for garnish, if desired. In a 3-quart saucepan, melt the butter over medium-high heat. Add the shelled shrimp and sauté until they turn pink. With a slotted spoon, remove them to a bowl. If you are using the unshelled shrimp, sauté them until they are tender and set them aside on a plate.

3. Stir the flour into the butter that remains in the saucepan. With a wire whisk, gradually stir in the milk until it is well blended. Cook over medium heat, stirring constantly, until the sauce thickens, about 5 minutes. Stir in the cheese, lemon juice, and mustard. Cover the sauce to keep it warm.

4. Remove the stems from the spinach leaves. Rinse the spinach well and drain thoroughly then coarsely chop. In a 5-quart Dutch oven, cook it with just the water clinging to its leaves until it is wilted, stirring frequently. Drain it in a colander and with the back of a spoon, press out as much moisture as possible. Place it in 4 individual ramekins or a large oval baking dish.

5. Shell the eggs and cut them into halves or quarters. Nestle the eggs in the spinach. Gently reheat the sauce over low heat and stir in the shelled shrimp. Add salt and pepper to taste. Spoon the sauce over the spinach and eggs. Garnish with reserved unshelled shrimp, if desired.

For a Puffy Souffle

Eggs are easiest to separate when they are refrigerator-cold, but will beat to greatest volume when they have been allowed to warm to room temperature. Even a tiny speck of yolk will retard the white's expanding, so do separate eggs carefully. A non-plastic, grease-free bowl will help whites to achieve the greatest volume.

Sonora Omelet

The Sonora desert spans northern Mexico and the southernmost part of America's Southwest. The food of the region is based on hot chilies, spiced meats, and large flour tortillas (rather than the more familiar corn tortillas). Serve this mildly spicy omelet with tortillas and, if the mood strikes, peppery Bloody Marys (page 188).

MAKES 2 SERVINGS

SALSA:
1 cup diced fresh or canned tomato
¼ cup chopped onion
¼ cup chopped canned green chilies
1 small clove garlic, minced
½ teaspoon salt

1 chorizo or 2 hot Italian sausages
4 large eggs
2 tablespoons milk
¼ teaspoon salt
2 tablespoons butter or margarine
½ cup shredded Monterey Jack or Cheddar cheese
½ cup sour cream
¼ cup chopped red onion
Shredded lettuce and sliced avocado

1. Several hours before serving or a day ahead, prepare the Salsa: Combine all the ingredients in a bowl. Cover and refrigerate.

2. If you are using chorizo, skin and finely chop it. Just skin Italian sausages. In a small skillet, fry the sausage, breaking it up with a spoon, until browned. Drain the sausage on paper towels.

3. In a medium-size bowl, beat the eggs, milk, and salt. In a 10-inch skillet or omelet pan, melt the butter over medium-high heat. Add the egg mixture and swirl the pan so that egg evenly covers the bottom. Cook until the eggs are almost firm but the top remains moist.

4. Spoon the sausage down the center of the eggs and sprinkle with the cheese. Fold the sides of the omelet up to almost enclose its filling.

5. Transfer the omelet to a serving plate. Top it with sour cream and onion, then garnish with lettuce and avocado. Serve the omelet with the salsa.

Mild Country Sausage, recipe page 108
Three Grain Pancakes, recipe page 74

Ramp-and-Potato Egg Scramble, page 88

Spring Greens Pie

Baked into an egg and cheese pie, young spring greens you pick yourself such as dandelion, beet, or spinach greens, lose any bitterness while bringing fresh flavor, pleasing texture, and great color. The pie's pastry is "baked blind"—that is, weighted with heavy dried beans or metal pellets, to prevent it from forming large bubbles.

MAKES 4 TO 6 SERVINGS

> Pastry for 1 piecrust
> 6 slices lean bacon
> 6 ounces (4 to 5 cups) tender dandelion greens, trimmed and rinsed
> 6 ounces (4 to 5 cups) young, fresh spinach or beet greens, trimmed and rinsed
> ¼ cup thinly sliced green onions
> 3 large eggs
> 1 large egg yolk
> 1 cup (½ pint) heavy cream or sour cream
> ¾ cup milk
> ¼ teaspoon dried basil
> ¼ teaspoon salt
> ⅛ teaspoon ground nutmeg
> Ground black pepper
> 1 large egg white, beaten (optional)
> ½ cup shredded Jarlsberg cheese
> 5 small green onions, blanched (optional)

1. Heat the oven to 375°F. Line a 9- or 10-inch quiche dish with the pastry. Line the pastry with waxed paper or aluminum foil and fill it with dried beans or rice, or aluminum pie pellets. Bake the piecrust 10 minutes, then remove it from the oven. Carefully remove the paper and beans from the piecrust.

2. In a large skillet, cook the bacon over medium heat until it is crisp. Drain it on paper towels. Pour off and discard all but 1 tablespoon of the bacon fat. Add the greens, spinach, and sliced green onions. Cook, stirring frequently, until the greens are wilted and no liquid remains, about 5 minutes.

3. In a large bowl, beat the eggs, yolk, cream, and milk. Stir in the basil, salt, nutmeg, and a pinch of pepper. If desired, brush the piecrust with a little egg white to help prevent sogginess.

4. Place the greens in the bottom of the crust; sprinkle with cheese and crumble bacon on top. Pour in the egg mixture. If desired, arrange blanched green onions on top and brush lightly with egg white.

5. Bake the pie 35 minutes, or until it is puffed and lightly browned. Its center should be slightly soft. If the green onions begin to brown on top, cover the quiche with aluminum foil during the last 15 minutes of baking. Remove the pie to a wire rack and let it stand 10 minutes before serving.

Sausage with Apples and Herbs, recipe page 110

Summer Garden Quiche

Take an early morning stroll to the garden and pick a ripe tomato and a shiny green pepper. Whisk them together with country eggs and sweet cream for a different, crustless quiche. If you want to make the quiche more substantial, toss in some smoky sausage or cooked ham.

MAKES 4 TO 6 SERVINGS

> 6 large eggs
> 1 pint heavy cream
> ½ teaspoon salt
> ¼ teaspoon ground white pepper
> Pinch of dried basil
> Pinch of dried thyme leaves
> ½ cup sliced fully-cooked, smoked
>   garlic sausage or diced ham
> ¼ cup chopped sweet green pepper
> ¼ cup chopped onion
> ¼ cup chopped tomato
> ¼ cup sliced fresh mushrooms
> ⅔ cup shredded Gruyère, Jarlsberg, or
>   Swiss cheese

1. Heat the oven to 350°F. Grease only the bottom of a 9- or 10-inch quiche dish.

2. In a medium-size bowl, mix the eggs, cream, salt, pepper, basil, and thyme until well blended.

3. In the greased dish, lightly toss the meat, green pepper, onion, tomato, and mushrooms until mixed. Sprinkle with the cheese. Pour the egg mixture over the vegetables and meat.

4. Bake the quiche 40 minutes, or until it is golden brown. The quiche is done when a knife inserted in center comes out clean. Let the quiche stand 10 minutes on a wire rack before serving.

Breakfast Frittata

In the sunny countries along the Mediterranean, cooks often serve frittatas—flat omelets cooked in large, cast-iron frying pans. Many are filled with bold vegetables such as tomatoes, peppers, and onions, and generously seasoned with fresh herbs. Our hearty frittata combines sweet sausage and potatoes.

MAKES 4 TO 6 SERVINGS

> 3 medium-size potatoes
> ½ pound country or sweet Italian sausages
> 6 large eggs
> ¼ cup milk
> 2 tablespoons chopped fresh parsley leaves
> ¼ teaspoon salt
> ¼ cup shredded mozzarella cheese

1. In a 2-quart saucepan, heat 2 inches water to boiling. Meanwhile, peel and slice the potatoes. Boil the potatoes just until fork-tender. Drain them.

2. Slice the sausages into ½-inch pieces. In a heavy 10-inch skillet with an oven-safe handle, sauté the sausage pieces, stirring occasionally, until they are cooked. Drain off the fat.

3. Add the potatoes to the sausage. In a large bowl, beat the eggs, milk, parsley, and salt. Pour the egg mixture over potatoes and sausage. Cover and cook over low heat 7 to 9 minutes, or until the center of the frittata is set.

4. Heat the broiler. Sprinkle the frittata with cheese. Broil the frittata 6 inches from the heat until the cheese is melted and lightly browned. Let the frittata stand 10 minutes on a wire rack. Cut into wedges and serve.

Fresh Asparagus Tart

Those first plucky spears of spring asparagus are a welcome sight, heralding the end of winter and promising gentler days. To celebrate their arrival, we've created a special tart for them.

MAKES 6 SERVINGS

> 1½ cups all-purpose flour
> ½ teaspoon salt
> 9 tablespoons butter, cut into small pieces
> About 5 tablespoons ice water
> 2 pounds asparagus
> 1½ cups half-and-half
> 3 large eggs
> Pinch of ground red pepper

1. In a food processor, with the chopping blade, combine the flour and ¼ teaspoon salt. Process 3 seconds to mix. Add the butter and process until the mixture resembles coarse crumbs. With the machine running, dribble in ice water until the mixture forms a dough that sticks to the blade. Remove the dough from the machine and knead gently 2 or 3 times. Sprinkle the dough with additional flour and wrap in waxed paper. Chill 30 minutes or up to 2 days.

2. Heat the oven to 375°F. Roll the dough out to a 13- by 9-inch rectangle or an 11-inch circle. Fit the dough into an 11- by 7-inch rectangular flan pan or a 9-inch quiche pan with a removable bottom. Pierce the pastry all over with a fork.

3. Line the pastry with waxed paper or aluminum foil and weigh down with uncooked dried beans or rice, or aluminum pie pellets. Bake the shell 15 minutes.

4. While the shell bakes, clean the asparagus. Steam or simmer it 5 to 8 minutes, until it is tender yet still crisp. Rinse it under cold water and dry thoroughly.

5. In a 1-quart saucepan, heat the half-and-half until bubbles form around the side of the pan. In a medium-size bowl, beat the eggs until they are frothy. Gradually beat in the half-and-half, the remaining ¼ teaspoon salt, and the pepper.

6. Remove the paper and beans from the tart shell. Arrange the asparagus spears in the shell. Carefully pour in the egg mixture.

7. Bake the tart 25 minutes, or until it is set and lightly browned. Let it stand 10 minutes on a wire rack before serving.

Buying Eggs

Eggs are graded and sized according to U.S. Department of Agriculture standards and most of the eggs in our markets are graded AA or A. When one of these eggs is cracked onto a plate, the yolk will hold its shape and the white will not be runny. As the grade goes down to B and C, the egg becomes thin and flat. Most of our recipes are developed with large eggs.

Meats

Bacon sizzling in the pan, ham quickly fried and served up with eggs-over-easy, a juicy rib-eye steak with creamy scrambled eggs, aromatic sausages browned to a turn—who said meat was not breakfast food? We consume more bacon than any other meat at breakfast time, frying it while the coffee brews. But as wonderful as bacon tastes, we ought not to neglect the other meats that taste mighty good first thing in the morning, too.

Many of the meats we associate with breakfast are salty or mildly spicy. Bacon, cured in brine and then smoked, is among the saltiest. Country ham is even saltier and must be soaked for hours before it is cooked. Once cooked and refrigerated, it keeps for weeks, ready to be sliced and eaten as wanted. Try not to buy a country ham that is already cooked. These hams tend to be tougher than the hams you take the time to prepare yourself. Country hams from Virginia and Kentucky are smoked as well as brine-cured. In the warmer regions of the deep South, the country hams are not smoked.

Canadian bacon is the brine-cured eye of the pork loin. Less fatty than other bacon (which is sliced from the fat-streaked belly of the hog), it is usually more thickly cut and the round slices are treated more as ham would be.

The best bacon is not terribly salty and is thick-cut with good broad streaks of meat interspersed with the fat. Cook bacon gently and watch it carefully to keep it from burning. Always drain it on paper towels before serving.

Besides pan frying, you can choose to broil, bake, or microwave bacon. To broil it, put in a single layer on the broiling pan and cook it about six inches from the heat source until it is crisp, usually three minutes or so. Turn it with tongs and cook it for one minute longer. To bake bacon, heat the oven to 450°F and lay a wire rack in a foil-lined jelly-roll pan.

Lay the strips of bacon on the rack, making sure a fat edge overlaps a lean one. There is no need to turn the bacon; it will be nice and brown in about ten minutes. Most of the fat will have collected in the bottom of the pan and so the bacon will not require a lot of draining. To microwave bacon, place four to six slices on top of four or five sheets of paper toweling. Cover with more towels and cook on high (100 percent) power until it is crisp, four to six minutes. Let the bacon stand for five minutes after taking it from the microwave to give it time to crisp.

Sausage is a great breakfast meat. If possible, buy yours from a butcher you like, or make it yourself. No need to stuff it into casings, unless you want to. Sausage meat can be made into patties and fried right away or frozen. When you are making sausage, particularly if you're using pork, taste test the mixture by frying a small patty—do not taste it raw.

In days gone by, we consumed great quantities of meat at the morning meal. Nowadays, we consider it an accompaniment to eggs, pancakes, and French toast. This way, we need eat only a small portion of fatty, salty bacon, rare steak, or corned beef hash. And so, even in this health-conscious era, there is no need to forsake the goodness of a country-style breakfast, complete with meat.

Country Ham with Redeye Gravy

(Photograph, Page 21)

Hardly a soul from Kentucky to Alabama needs a recipe for this item. A generous slice of cured country ham is browned in a little fat, lifted from the pan, and then the "gravy" is made by stirring the pan drippings with a little water and good, strong coffee from the morning pot. The coffee gives the gravy a slightly reddish tone, hence the name.

MAKES 2 OR 3 SERVINGS

> 1 large, ½-inch-thick center slice boiled
> or baked country ham
> ⅔ cup hot water
> 2 tablespoons strong black coffee

1. Trim off some of the fat around the edge of the ham slice, if desired, and reserve. Slash the remaining fat around the edge to prevent curling.

2. Very lightly oil a large skillet, or cook some of the trimmed fat a few minutes over low heat. Add the ham and cook over medium-low heat for 10 to 15 minutes, turning 3 or 4 times, until it is heated through and lightly browned around the edges.

3. Remove the ham to a heated platter and pour the water and coffee into the skillet. Increase the heat to medium-high and simmer 3 to 5 minutes, stirring to incorporate all the pan drippings, until the gravy is reddish and slightly reduced.

Corned Beef Hash with Eggs

(Photograph, Page 61)

Corned beef hash is a tradition in the kitchens of New England, whether they're found in farmhouses snuggled in the green valleys of Vermont or in old clapboard houses perched above the rocky shores of Maine. Originally devised as a way to use leftover New England boiled dinner, corned beef hash is worth your time to make from scratch. Paired with fried eggs, and served with Grilled Sticky Buns (page 131), it is a breakfast hard to surpass.

MAKES 4 SERVINGS

> 2 tablespoons butter or margarine
> 1 pound all-purpose potatoes, peeled and
> cut into ½-inch cubes
> 1 large onion, coarsely chopped
> ¼ teaspoon salt
> ⅛ teaspoon ground black pepper
> 1 pound cooked corned beef, cut into
> ½-inch cubes
> 4 to 8 large eggs

1. In a large skillet, melt 1 tablespoon butter. Add the potatoes, onion, salt, and pepper. Cover the skillet and cook, stirring frequently, until the potatoes are almost tender, about 10 minutes.

2. Stir the corned beef into the potato mixture. Cook, uncovered, over medium heat, until the corned beef has heated through and any liquid in the pan has evaporated, about 15 minutes.

3. In another skillet, melt half the remaining butter. Fry the eggs to order, adding more butter when necessary.

4. To serve, spoon the hash onto individual plates. Top with fried eggs.

Turkey Sausage

No longer relegated to winter holidays, turkey is showing up at family meals more and more often. Don't exclude this lean meat from the breakfast table—make ground turkey sausages pleasantly seasoned with thyme, sage, and allspice. These do not have the fat that pork sausages do and so be careful that they do not become dry from overcooking.

MAKES 12 PATTIES

> 1 cup fresh bread crumbs (2 slices bread)
> ½ cup milk
> 2 pounds fresh or thawed frozen ground raw turkey
> ½ cup chopped fresh parsley leaves
> 2 teaspoons dried thyme leaves
> 1 teaspoon salt
> 1 teaspoon dried rubbed sage
> ¼ teaspoon ground black pepper
> ⅛ teaspoon ground allspice
> About 3 tablespoons butter or vegetable oil, for frying

1. In a medium-size bowl, combine the bread crumbs and milk; let stand 5 minutes to soften the crumbs. With a fork, stir in the turkey, parsley, thyme, salt, sage, pepper, and allspice.

2. Divide the mixture into 12 portions and shape each into a 2¾-inch patty. Place the patties on a tray; cover them and refrigerate at least 1 hour or overnight to blend the flavors.

3. To serve, in a large skillet, heat 1 tablespoon butter and fry the patties, half at a time, until they are browned on both sides, adding more butter when necessary.

Pork and Grits Hash

To get a windy March day off to a good start, try this robust hash made with grits and chunks of leftover pork. When the grits have been made ahead, the hash can be cooked up in minutes. It tastes especially good with a spoonful or two of your favorite sweet pepper relish.

MAKES 6 SERVINGS

> 3 cups water
> ¾ cup quick-cooking grits
> ¾ teaspoon salt
> 1 tablespoon butter or margarine
> ½ cup coarsely chopped onion
> 2 cups cubed cooked pork
> ¼ teaspoon dried basil
> ¼ teaspoon dried thyme leaves

1. Several hours or the night before serving, prepare the grits: In a heavy 2-quart saucepan, heat 2¼ cups water to boiling over high heat. In a small bowl, combine the grits, ½ teaspoon salt, and remaining ¾ cup water. Stir the grits mixture into the boiling water. Cook, stirring constantly, until the grits are thickened and bubbly, about 5 minutes. Cover and cook over low heat 5 minutes.

2. Generously grease an 8-inch-square baking pan. Pour the grits into the greased pan. Cool to room temperature, then cover tightly and refrigerate until the grits are is firm, several hours or overnight.

3. About 20 minutes before serving, cut the grits into ½-inch squares. In a large skillet, melt the butter. Add the grits, onion, pork, basil, thyme, and remaining ¼ teaspoon salt. Sauté, stirring constantly, until the onion is well browned. Serve immediately.

Mild Country Sausage

(Photograph, Page 97)

There are a number of tasty sausages available in the markets, but you won't be surprised to find that homemade tastes best. With a food processor or meat grinder, making sausage is surprisingly easy. Be sure to add as much fat as called for. Fat is integral to sausage-making, keeping the sausages moist as they cook. To test for seasoning, fry a small patty, and taste it—never taste-test raw sausage meat. A sausage roll, tightly wrapped, will keep in the refrigerator a few days, and in the freezer up to three months.

MAKES 10 TO 12 SLICES

> 1 pound boneless lean pork
> 6 to 8 ounces pork fat
> 1½ teaspoons coarse salt
> 1 teaspoon dried rubbed sage
> 1 teaspoon dried summer savory
> ½ teaspoon dried thyme leaves
> ¼ teaspoon freshly ground black pepper
> ⅛ teaspoon crushed red pepper

1. If you are using a food processor, cut the pork into 1-inch cubes and chop the fat into ½-inch pieces. For a meat grinder, cut both into 3- by ½-inch strips. Chill the pork and fat in the freezer just until they are firm but not frozen.

2. While the meat chills, in a large bowl, combine the salt, sage, savory, thyme, and peppers.

3. Add the pork and fat to the seasonings; toss until they are well mixed. In a food processor, with the chopping blade, process the meat mixture, half at a time, until it is coarsely ground. If you are using a meat grinder, grind the mixture through the coarse blade. Cover the sausage and refrigerate it 12 to 24 hours to blend the flavors.

4. Dip your hands in ice water and shape the sausage into an 8-inch cylinder. Cut the sausage into ½-inch slices and place them in a cold skillet. Cook the sausage slices over medium heat until they are well browned but not crisp. Pour off the fat as necessary. Drain the sausage on paper towels and serve.

Farm-Style Sausage Patties

This sausage is seasoned a little differently from Mild Country Sausage (left). It is flavored with garlic, cloves, and allspice, and tastes perfect with a couple of eggs-over-easy and toasted home-baked bread. Salt pork and side pork are from the belly of the hog, as is bacon, but salt pork is brine-cured only, and not smoked. Side pork is not cured or smoked. Side or salt pork often has no or very few streaks of meat in the fat, yet still gives sausage flavor and the necessary measure of moistness.

MAKES ABOUT 16 PATTIES

> 2½ pounds boneless pork butt or shoulder
> ½ pound salt pork or unsalted side pork,
>   skinned if necessary
> 2 to 3 teaspoons salt
> 1 tablespoon dried rubbed sage
> 1½ teaspoons coarsely ground black pepper
> ¾ teaspoon ground cloves
> ¼ teaspoon dried thyme leaves
> ¼ teaspoon ground allspice
> 1 medium-size onion, minced
> 1 clove garlic, minced

1.   If you are using a food processor, cut the pork into 1-inch cubes and the salt pork into ½-inch pieces. For a meat grinder, cut both into 3- by ½-inch strips. Chill the meat in freezer, just until it is firm but not frozen.

2.   While the meat chills, in a large bowl, combine 2 teaspoons salt, the sage, pepper, cloves, thyme, allspice, onion, and garlic.

3.   Add the meat to the seasonings and toss until they are well mixed. In a food processor, with the chopping blade, process the meat mixture, a small amount at a time, until it is coarsely ground. If you are using a meat grinder, grind the mixture through the coarse blade. Make a small patty and cook it in a skillet; taste and add more salt or seasonings, if desired. Cover the sausage and refrigerate it 12 to 24 hours to blend the flavors.

4.   Dip your hands in ice water and shape the sausage into 2½-inch patties. Cook the patties in a large skillet over medium heat until they are well browned but not crisp. Pour off the fat as necessary. Drain the sausage on paper towels and serve.

Scrapple

Thrifty Pennsylvania Dutch farmwives never let a bit of the hog go unused when butchering time came around each fall. They used the leftover "scraps" to make scrapple, a mixture of pork and cornmeal which is shaped into a loaf so that slices can be cut as needed and quickly fried in a hot skillet. This recipe is more realistic for today's cooks, relying on mildly seasoned ground pork mixed with cornmeal to form the loaf. Fried for breakfast, scrapple is most delicious when pure maple syrup is poured over it.

MAKES 8 SERVINGS

> **1 pound ground pork**
> **5 cups water**
> **1 teaspoon salt**
> **½ to 1 teaspoon ground black pepper**
> **¼ teaspoon dried rubbed sage**
> **2 cups white cornmeal**
> **¼ cup (½ stick) butter or vegetable**
>   **shortening**
> **½ cup maple or golden syrup**

1.   In a 5-quart saucepot, gently sauté the ground pork until it loses its pinkness. Add 3 cups water, the salt, pepper to taste, and sage. Heat to boiling; cover and simmer over low heat 30 minutes.

2.   Pour the mixture into a food processor and with the chopping blade, process until the pork is finely chopped. Return to the pot. In a bowl, combine the cornmeal and remaining 2 cups water. Stir the cornmeal mixture into the pork mixture. Heat to boiling over medium-high heat, stirring constantly. Reduce the heat to low; cover, and cook gently 15 minutes, stirring occasionally to prevent sticking.

3.   Meanwhile, generously oil a loaf pan. Pour the scrapple into the pan and spread to make the top level. Cool it to room temperature, then cover and refrigerate overnight.

4.   To serve, unmold the loaf and cut it into 16 slices. In a large skillet, heat 1 tablespoon butter and fry the slices, several at a time, until they are browned on both sides. Add more butter when necessary. Serve the fried scrapple with syrup.

Sausage with Apples and Herbs

(Photograph, page 100)

Thank goodness for apples—they are wonderful eaten out of hand, baked into mouth-watering pies and especially, cooked up with any number of meats. For a snappy breakfast that really isn't much work, try these sausages and apples.

MAKES 4 SERVINGS

> 2 large cooking apples
> 1 tablespoon unsalted butter
> 1 pound large sausage links
> 1 clove garlic, peeled
> 1 sprig fresh rosemary
> 2 fresh sage leaves
> 1½ cups sweet apple cider or natural apple juice

1. Peel, core, and cut the apples into rings. In a large skillet, melt the butter over medium heat. Add the apple rings and sauté just until they soften slightly. Remove them to a plate and keep them warm.

2. In the same skillet, fry the sausage links, turning them frequently, until they are golden-brown. Pour off and discard the fat. Add the garlic, rosemary, and sage to the pan and pour in the cider. Heat the cider to boiling and continue to cook it, bubbling gently, until the liquid has almost evaporated and the sausages are cooked through.

3. Turn the sausages occasionally and add more cider if the pan begins to dry out. You should have just a few spoonfuls of syrupy liquid. Return the apple rings to the skillet to reheat and serve.

Ham and Grits Loaf

Pale pink ham and creamy grits make this layered casserole as pretty as it is tasty. Try it with scrambled eggs and a basket of Rye Biscuits (page 25) or Savory Cheddar Muffins (page 38).

MAKES 6 SERVINGS

> 2 cups water
> ½ cup quick-cooking grits
> ¼ teaspoon salt
> ½ cup milk
> 1 large egg
> 1 tablespoon ketchup
> ⅛ teaspoon ground black pepper
> 1 cup fresh bread crumbs (2 slices bread)
> ¾ pound boiled ham, ground
> ½ pound ground beef
> ¼ cup finely chopped onion
> ¼ cup chopped fresh parsley leaves

1. In a heavy 2-quart saucepan, heat 1½ cups water to boiling over high heat. In a small bowl, combine the grits, salt, and remaining ½ cup water. Stir the grits mixture into the boiling water. Cook, stirring constantly, until the mixture is thickened and bubbly, about 5 minutes. Cover and cook over low heat 5 minutes.

2. Heat the oven to 350°F. In a medium-size bowl, combine the milk, egg, ketchup, and pepper. Stir in the bread crumbs and let stand 5 minutes. Stir the ham, beef, onion, and parsley into the bread crumb mixture.

3. Generously grease a loaf pan. Spoon half the ham mixture into the pan. Top with half the grits mixture, the remaining ham and the remaining grits.

4. Bake the loaf 50 to 55 minutes, or until the center feels firm when gently touched. Let the loaf cool 5 minutes on a wire rack, then remove it from the pan. Carefully cut it into slices and serve.

Country Terrine

We tend to think of terrines and pâtés (which are, essentially, the same thing) as elegant fare, to be eaten only on the fanciest occasions. The fact is that terrines such as this one, made with ground pork and a judicious amount of herbs, are economical and easy dishes, fine with homemade breads and biscuits, crocks of creamery butter, and a tray of well-aged cheeses.

MAKES 10 SERVINGS

> 1½ pounds boneless pork cubes or ground
>   pork
> 2 tablespoons grated lemon rind
> 2 tablespoons lemon juice
> 5 cloves garlic, finely chopped
> 1½ teaspoons dried thyme leaves
> 1¼ teaspoons salt
> 1 teaspoon ground coriander
> ¼ teaspoon ground black pepper
> 2 10-ounce packages frozen leaf spinach
> 6 slices bacon
> Parsley sprigs (optional)

1. In a food processor, with the chopping blade, combine the pork, lemon rind and juice, garlic, thyme, salt, coriander, and pepper. Process until the mixture is finely ground. Cover tightly and refrigerate at least 2 to 4 hours.

2. Just before baking, in a 2-quart saucepan, cook the spinach following package directions, but omit any salt. Drain the spinach well and squeeze it dry. Coarsely chop it and fold it into the meat mixture.

3. Heat the oven to 325°F. Lightly oil a 1½-quart round or oval terrine. Arrange 3 slices bacon in the bottom. Pack in the meat-and-spinach mixture. Arrange the remaining 3 slices bacon on top, crossing them in the center. Cover the terrine tightly with oiled aluminum foil.

4. Bake the terrine 1½ hours, or until a meat thermometer inserted in the center registers 170°F and the juices are clear.

5. Cool the terrine 30 minutes on a wire rack. Pour off and discard the juices. Cover the terrine tightly and refrigerate at least 6 hours or overnight. To serve, garnish with parsley, if desired.

Finishing Terrines

A baked terrine slices more easily if it has been weighted down while it is refrigerated. After the terrine has baked and cooled, cover it with aluminum foil. Place a plate or a piece of heavy cardboard on top and weight the meat with heavy cans or jars. After chilling, the baked terrine will have a smooth, compressed texture.

Cereals, Grains & Potatoes

Hot cereal on a winter's day is so thoroughly satisfying that when we spy the familiar round oatmeal box in the cupboard in blazing July, we stop for a moment to remember snow-covered fields and warm, cozy kitchens. Setting bowls of oatmeal, cream of wheat or farina before our children on a January morning makes us feel better about sending them out to the side of the road to wait for the school bus. We, ourselves, might indulge in honey-sweetened hot cereal on a blustery Saturday morning, shoring up energy for the household tasks we have set for the day.

A valuable source of fiber and nutrients, grains have long been a vital part of man's diet. They have been ground into flour for baking since ancient times, and for just as long have been eaten as hot cereal—also called mush or gruel. Far more recently, grains were converted into flakes and puffs to be eaten as cold cereal. The process for doing this was developed in Battle Creek, Michigan, and what began as an experiment in a new sort of health food has grown into a billion dollar industry.

Grains are the dried seeds of grass-like plants. The most familiar are wheat, rice, oats, corn, rye, barley, buckwheat, and millet. All can be eaten hot as cereal simply by boiling them. Many are precooked so that they are easier to prepare.

Oats are usually steamed to soften them and then rolled into flaky particles. The only difference between old-fashioned and quick oats is the thickness and size of the flakes. Steel-cut oats, also called Scotch or Irish oatmeal, are small-cut oat grains with a nuttier flavor than rolled oats. They are easiest to find in natural food stores.

Wheat kernels or berries require several hours of cooking. When the wheat berries are ground into meal they are called cream of wheat or farina. When wheat berries are cooked, dried, and cracked, they are called bulgur. Wheat flakes, made by rolling softened wheat berries, are similar in appearance to old-fashioned oats and should not be confused with ready-to-eat wheat-flake cereal.

Cornmeal, which lends its good flavor to muffins, quick breads, and flapjacks, is made from ground, dried white or yellow corn kernels. Grits are less coarsely ground than meal, and corn flour is more finely ground.

Whether you prefer hearty oatmeal or smooth cream of wheat, cold weather breakfasts would not be the same without hot cereals. Try them, too, in the warmer months. They are delicious topped with fresh berries and other summer fruit.

Potatoes are one vegetable we would have a hard time living without. These mild tubers are welcome at any meal, and often in-between in the form of snacks such as chips and fries. Hash browns and potato pancakes are happy visions on the breakfast table. Warm and crusty, begging to be paired with fried eggs or perhaps some freshly made applesauce, everyone adores them. Potatoes are available all year long, but are at their very best, not surprisingly, in late summer when you dig them from your own garden.

Crunchy Almond Granola

(Photograph, page 80)

Granola, a favorite snack of lunchbox-toting children, is terrific for breakfast, too. Toss a handful on the morning oatmeal or yogurt, or serve it with fresh fruit and milk. This baked version is similar to packaged granolas, at a fraction of their cost.

MAKES ABOUT 10 CUPS

> 5 cups old-fashioned rolled oats
>   (about 1 pound)
> 2 cups wheat bran cereal
> 1 cup blanched whole or slivered almonds
> ½ cup sunflower seeds
> 1 teaspoon ground cinnamon
> ½ cup honey
> ½ cup sunflower or corn oil
> 1 cup dark seedless raisins (optional)

1. Heat the oven to 300°F. Line a large, shallow roasting pan with aluminum foil. In a large bowl, combine the oats, bran cereal, almonds, sunflower seeds, and cinnamon.

2. In a 1-quart saucepan, heat the honey and oil just until bubbles appear around the side of the pan. Pour the honey mixture over the oat mixture and toss until well combined.

3. Spread the granola evenly in the foil-lined pan. Bake 40 to 50 minutes, or until the cereal is golden, stirring it every 10 minutes. Stir in the raisins, if desired. Cool and store in an airtight container.

Homemade Muesli

(Photograph, page 80)

Eat this muesli after it has had a short soak in milk or cream. It's particularly tasty for breakfast at a campsite or on a road trip, particularly for those days when you get an early start.

MAKES 8 CUPS

> 2¼ cups old-fashioned rolled oats
> 1½ cups (rolled) barley flakes
> 1½ cups (rolled) wheat flakes
> 1 cup dark seedless raisins
> ½ cup coarsely chopped dried apple
> ½ cup unprocessed oat bran
> ½ cup wheat germ
> ¼ cup chopped almonds or hazelnuts
> 3 tablespoons light-brown sugar

In a large bowl, mix all the ingredients. Store the muesli in an airtight container.

Grain Cereal With Apricots and Pistachios

Inspired by the fertile farms of the Great Plains, we've created a hot cereal that combines steel-cut oats, wheat flakes, and bran. For extra goodness, mineral-rich apricots, raisins, and pistachio nuts are sprinkled over the cereal just before serving. Buy natural, unsalted pistachios for this recipe.

MAKES 6 SERVINGS

> 4 cups water
> 1 cup steel-cut oats
> 1 cup (rolled) wheat flakes
> ½ cup unprocessed oat bran
> ¼ teaspoon salt
> ¼ teaspoon ground nutmeg
> 1½ to 2 cups apple juice
> ¼ cup slivered dried apricots
> ¼ cup unsalted pistachio nuts, coarsely chopped
> ¼ cup dark seedless raisins
> 1 tablespoon sugar

1.   In a heavy 2-quart saucepan, heat the water to boiling over high heat. Stir in the oats, wheat, bran, salt, and nutmeg. Cover and cook the cereal over medium-low heat, stirring occasionally, until it is thick, about 15 minutes.

2.   Stir 1½ cups apple juice into the cereal. Continue to cook the mixture until it is creamy, about 5 minutes. Add more apple juice if you prefer a softer consistency.

3.   Meanwhile, in a small bowl, combine the apricots, nuts, raisins, and sugar. Ladle the hot cereal into individual serving bowls. Sprinkle the fruit-and-nut mixture over the cereal and serve immediately, with milk or cream, if desired.

Apple and Pineapple Muesli
(Photograph, page 80)

Muesli, the invention of a Swiss nutritionist, is a mixture of uncooked rolled oats that have been moistened with water and, often, nuts and dried fruit. Just before it is eaten, milk or cream and fresh fruit are stirred into this healthful concoction. Our version differs a bit from the original formula, as it is moistened with apple juice, yogurt, and milk, then sweetened with honey.

MAKES 4 SERVINGS

> 1 cup quick rolled oats
> ½ cup apple juice
> 1 8-ounce can crushed pineapple in juice
> 1 small red apple
> 1 8-ounce container vanilla-flavored yogurt

1.   In a medium-size bowl, combine the oats, apple juice, and crushed pineapple with its juice. Cover and refrigerate the muesli several hours or overnight.

2.   Just before serving, coarsely shred the apple. Stir the apple and yogurt into the muesli. Serve with milk and honey or brown sugar, if desired.

Breakfast Grits

(Photograph, page 21)

To folks from the Deep South, the title of this recipe may be redundant: grits are for breakfast. Grits are (some people say "is") mild breakfast cereal that is made from ground corn and needs only a melting pat of butter. Grits also stand up just fine to Country Ham with Redeye Gravy (page 106). Be sure not to use "quick-cooking grits" for this recipe.

MAKES 6 SERVINGS

> 5 cups water
> 2 teaspoons salt
> 1 cup regular grits
> ¼ cup light cream or milk
> Pinch of ground black pepper
> 2 tablespoons butter

1. In a heavy 2-quart saucepan, heat the water to boiling over high heat. Reduce the heat to medium and add the salt. Pour the grits into the water in a fine steady stream, stirring constantly.

2. Reduce the heat to low, then cover and cook until the water is absorbed and grits are thick but still creamy, about 15 minutes. Meanwhile, heat the cream until it is just warm. Stir the cream and pepper into the grits. If the grits are lumpy, beat them briefly with a wire whisk. Remove the pan from the heat.

3. Cover and let the grits stand 2 minutes. They may be kept warm in the top of a double boiler over simmering water, but they are best served immediately. If they thicken, stir in a little more cream or milk. Top each serving with a small pat of butter.

Cheddar Cheese Grits

(Photograph, back jacket)

In some parts of the country, cheese and grits are as common a pairing at breakfast as ham and eggs. Later in the day they make a hearty side dish for chicken or pork, but do try them first thing in the morning, when they don't have to play second fiddle to anything else on the table.

MAKES 6 SERVINGS

> 3¾ cups water
> 1 cup quick-cooking grits
> 1 teaspoon salt
> ¼ teaspoon ground black pepper
> ½ cup milk
> 1 large egg
> 1 cup shredded Cheddar cheese

1. In a heavy 2-quart saucepan, heat 3 cups water to boiling over high heat. In a small bowl, combine the grits, salt, pepper, and remaining ¾ cup water. Stir the grits mixture into the boiling water. Cook, stirring constantly, until the mixture is thickened and bubbly, about 5 minutes. Cover and cook over low heat 5 minutes.

2. Heat the oven to 400°F. Grease a 1½-quart baking dish. In a cup, beat together the milk and the egg. Fold the milk mixture and ½ cup cheese into the grits. Turn the mixture into the greased baking dish. Top with the remaining cheese.

3. Bake the grits 25 to 30 minutes, or until the cheese is bubbly and browned.

Cranberry and Almond Muffins, recipe page 36
Cranberry Braid, recipe page 142
(Overleaf)
Pecan Coffee Ring, recipe page 144

Pennsylvania Dutch Apple-Muffin Cake, page 140

Elvin's Fried Grits

Deep-fried grits, cooked to a golden turn, are a delightfully unexpected addition to nearly any breakfast, particularly one where meat, eggs, or tomatoes figure on the menu. These earned their reputation for excellence at Tujague's, a New Orleans restaurant.

MAKES 8 SERVINGS

4 cups water
1¾ cups milk
¼ cup (½ stick) butter or margarine
1½ teaspoons sugar
1 teaspoon salt
2 cups quick-cooking grits

BATTER:
1½ cups all-purpose flour
½ cup packaged seasoned bread crumbs
1 teaspoon dried parsley flakes
3 large eggs
¼ cup milk

¾ cup vegetable oil, for frying

1. In a heavy 4-quart saucepan, combine 2½ cups water, the milk, butter, sugar, and salt. Heat to boiling over high heat. In a small bowl, combine the grits and remaining 1½ cups water. Stir the grits mixture into the boiling milk mixture. Cook, stirring constantly, until the mixture is thickened and bubbly, about 5 minutes. Cover and cook over low heat 5 minutes.

2. Grease a loaf pan. Pour the grits mixture into the greased pan and cool to room temperature. Cover the pan with aluminum foil and refrigerate until the grits are firm, several hours or overnight.

3. Prepare the Batter: In a large bowl, combine the flour, bread crumbs, and parsley. In a medium-size bowl, beat the eggs and milk. Unmold the grits loaf and cut it into 16 slices.

4. In a large skillet, heat the vegetable oil over high heat. Dip the grits slices in the flour mixture, then in the beaten eggs, then again in the flour. Fry the slices in the oil, a few at a time, turning occasionally, until they are golden brown. Drain them on paper towels and serve hot.

Downhome Rice Porridge

If someone in your family cannot digest milk, try this unusual hot, savory cereal made with broth. Breakfast in China is frequently a bowl of rice porridge topped with tidbits of meat or pickled vegetables. Here in America, we add slivers of ham and chopped green onion. For convenience, the porridge can be cooked ahead, cooled and refrigerated, then reheated.

MAKES 4 SERVINGS

> ⅔ **cup short-grain brown rice**
> 2¾ **cups water**
> 1 13¾- **or** 14½-**ounce can chicken broth**
> ½ **teaspoon Worcestershire sauce**
> 1 **tablespoon vegetable oil**
> 2 **large eggs, beaten**
> 1 **cup slivered cooked ham**
> 2 **tablespoons chopped green onion**
>   **(optional)**

1. In a 4-quart saucepan, heat the rice, water, and chicken broth to boiling over high heat. Reduce the heat to low; cover the pan and simmer the rice mixture 1½ to 2 hours, or until it is thick and soupy. Stir the cereal occasionally to prevent it from sticking to the pan. Stir in the Worcestershire sauce.

2. In a large skillet, heat the oil over medium heat. Add half the eggs and cook without stirring just until they are set into a "pancake." With a pancake turner, turn the pancake over and cook it a few seconds longer. Transfer it to a cutting board and repeat with the remaining beaten eggs. Cut the egg pancakes into 3- by ½-inch strips.

3. In the same skillet, cook the ham slivers until they are heated through. Spoon the porridge into serving bowls and top with the egg strips, ham, and chopped green onion.

Spoon Bread

Hot and golden from the oven, spoon bread has been gracing the breakfast tables of the South for years. A cross between a souffle and cornbread, the soft, slightly sweet dish goes well with ham and eggs, sausage, or broiled tomatoes. Like a souffle, spoon bread should be served as soon as it's taken from the oven.

MAKES 6 SERVINGS

> 1½ **cups water**
> 1¼ **cups white cornmeal**
> 1 **tablespoon sugar**
> 1 **teaspoon salt**
> 3 **large eggs**
> 1 **tablespoon butter**
> 1 **cup buttermilk**
> ½ **teaspoon baking soda**

1. In a 2-quart saucepan, heat 1 cup water to boiling over high heat. In a small bowl, combine the cornmeal, sugar, salt, and remaining ½ cup water. Pour the cornmeal mixture into boiling water. Cook the mixture over medium heat, stirring constantly, until it is thickened and bubbly, about 5 minutes. Remove from the heat and allow to cool to warm.

2. Meanwhile, separate the eggs, placing the whites in a medium-size bowl and adding the yolks to the cornmeal mixture. Let the whites warm to room temperature. Stir the butter, buttermilk, and baking soda into the cornmeal mixture.

3. Heat the oven to 350°F. Grease a 1½-quart baking dish or casserole. With an electric mixer at high speed, beat the whites until stiff peaks form. With a rubber spatula, gently fold the whites into the cornmeal mixture until no streaks of white remain.

4. Pour the batter into the greased baking dish. Bake 45 to 50 minutes, or until the spoon bread is golden brown and puffy. Serve immediately.

Home Fries with Carrots

Heartier than other potato side dishes, this vegetable casserole is recommended for winter's most blustery mornings. Allow a half hour baking time.

MAKES 8 SERVINGS

    3 tablespoons butter or margarine
    3 tablespoons olive oil
    6 medium-size (about 2 pounds), all-purpose
        potatoes, peeled and thinly sliced
    1 pound carrots, peeled and sliced
    2 medium-size onions, thinly sliced
    ½ teaspoon salt

1. Heat the oven to 400°F. In a large skillet, preferably with a non-stick surface, heat half the butter and oil. Add half the potatoes, carrots, and onions, and sauté until the potatoes are tender-crisp, about 10 minutes. Transfer the vegetables to a 13-by 9-inch baking pan. Repeat with the remaining vegetables.

2. Sprinkle the vegetables with salt. Bake them 30 minutes, or until they are crisp and golden brown.

Hash Brown Potatoes

(Photograph, page 79)

Created by short-order cooks for last night's leftover boiled potatoes, hash browns are the crispy, fried potatoes served up in diners and coffee shops across the country every morning. Though there are as many variations as there are cooks, the original recipe called for a mound of shredded potatoes that was fried on a griddle, weighted with a heavy press to speed its cooking. As the potatoes fried, they cooked into a crusty cake. Hash browns are traditionally served with ketchup.

MAKES 4 SERVINGS

    4 to 5 tablespoons vegetable oil
    4 cups coarsely shredded, peeled, boiled
        baking potatoes
    ½ teaspoon salt

1. In a 10-inch skillet or on a griddle, heat 2 tablespoons oil over medium-high heat. Add two 1-cup mounds of potatoes and, with a large pancake turner, shape each into a rectangle about ¾-inch thick.

2. Press the mounds to make the potatoes stick together; fry until the bottoms are crisp, about 8 to 10 minutes. Sprinkle the potatoes lightly with salt. Turn and brown the other side, adding more oil if necessary. Transfer the hash browns to serving plates and cook the remaining potatoes.

Chunky Hash Browns

Unlike Hash Browns (page 123), these are made with large chunks of potatoes and are not fried to a crisp finish. Paprika adds color to potatoes that are only lightly browned, and onion and green pepper give them a flavor that calls out for eggs any style.

MAKES 4 SERVINGS

> 4 medium-size (about 1¼ pounds)
>   all-purpose potatoes
> 3 tablespoons bacon fat or vegetable oil
> 1 small onion, sliced or chopped
> ½ small green pepper, seeded and diced
> ½ teaspoon salt
> ½ teaspoon paprika
> ⅛ teaspoon ground black pepper

1. Place the potatoes in a 2-quart saucepan and add cold water to cover. Heat to boiling over high heat. Reduce the heat to medium, then cover and cook the potatoes just until they are tender, about 20 minutes. Drain the potatoes, cool, and refrigerate until they are cold.

2. Peel the potatoes, and cut each into quarters, then into ½-inch-thick slices.

3. In a large skillet, heat the fat over medium heat. Add the potatoes, onion, green pepper, salt, paprika, and pepper. Cook, stirring occasionally, until the onion and green pepper are tender and the potatoes are lightly browned, about 15 minutes.

Potato Pancakes

Crisp, freshly made potato pancakes are one of our most enduring recipes. Called "latkes" in the Jewish tradition and customarily served at holiday time, the pancakes go well with sour cream and applesauce. They are always made from raw potatoes.

MAKES ABOUT 6 SERVINGS

> 3 large eggs
> 6 large all-purpose potatoes, peeled
> 1 large onion
> 1 teaspoon salt
> ⅛ teaspoon ground black pepper
> 1 cup vegetable oil, for frying

1. Separate the eggs, placing the whites in a medium-size bowl and the yolks in a cup. Let them warm to room temperature.

2. Into a large bowl, finely grate the potatoes and onion. Add cold water to cover to keep the potatoes from discoloring.

3. Thoroughly drain the potato mixture, squeezing it dry between your hands. Return it to the bowl and stir in the yolks, salt, and pepper. With an electric mixer on high speed, beat the whites until stiff peaks form. Gently fold the whites into the potato mixture.

4. In a large skillet, heat ¼ inch oil until hot over medium heat. Drop rounded tablespoonfuls of the potato mixture into the hot oil, and with a pancake turner or metal spatula, flatten them to make thin pancakes. Fry the pancakes slowly, turning once, until they are crisp and golden brown. Drain them on a baking sheet lined with paper towels and keep them warm in a low oven while frying the rest.

From the Morning Pantry

Besides these recipes for eggs and meats, cereals and baked treats, there are other, less traditional dishes that can comprise a healthful, satisfying breakfast. On winter's raw mornings, soup is marvelously comforting. Conversely, hazy summer mornings sing out for salads, full of leafy green goodness.

On almost any day, cheese and fruit are a glorious beginning. Depending on personal preference and the season, the cheese may be a tangy chèvre, a pungent Gruyère, or even an eye-opening Stilton accompanied by soft fruit—dark berries, green and red grapes, sweet plums—or more exotic luxuries like pineapples, mangos, and papayas. Almost any fruit can be baked, too. Add a little brown sugar to pineapple cubes and set them in the oven, or try pears or bananas; the versatile apple is also good poached.

Sandwiches can be hearty and easy breakfasts. A BLT, ham and cheese on whole-wheat bread, or a fried egg sandwich—all are filling morning meals that don't require too much preparation time.

For many, seafood makes a perfect weekend breakfast. It's also an easy one. You can get smoked fish at the delicatessen—whitefish, halibut, cod, and, of course, lox (smoked salmon). Serve it with bagels, onions, tomatoes, and cream cheese, to which you can add your favorite flavorings—fresh-snipped chives, sliced green onions, or chopped celery and carrots. Smoked kippers are synonymous with breakfast in many parts of Great Britain and are carried in specialty stores here. The smoky flavor can really wake up your taste buds. Other smoked fish such as trout, mackerel, or even catfish may be harder to find, but worth trying for a deliciously different breakfast.

Buns, Pastries & Coffeecakes

Warm, comforting, honest-to-goodness breakfast cakes and pastries seem almost to spill forth from the country kitchen redolent with the good smells of baking: fresh dough, cinnamon, brown sugar, and homegrown fruit. The image of a pan of hot buns being lifted from the deep black of the oven, held aloft with a large thick dish towel doubling for a potholder as it's carried to the broad table in the middle of the room, is perhaps a romantic one that harks back to our rural roots. Fantasy or reality, it is an image which makes us yearn for simpler times when the food was good and plain, the company loving.

Yet whether we grew up on a farm or in a city apartment, nearly everyone shares memories of childhood breakfasts filled with freshly baked buns, pastries and coffeecakes. In some households, Sunday morning was the time for a special coffeecake; in others, they were saved for holidays such as Christmas. Some of our mothers baked them to share with friends over morning coffee and gossip — and we hoped there would be some left when we got home from school.

While many pastries, including croissants, are gifts from Europe, coffeecakes, and to a slightly lesser degree buns, are an American institution. We truly enjoy something sweet with our coffee and cross all ethnic boundaries when it comes to making sweet cakes for the morning meal. These are deceptively plain looking creations, rich with butter, eggs, sugar, fruit and nuts, flavored with citrus, cinnamon, and spices. They may be topped with crumbly streusel, a dusting of confectioners' sugar or a simple sugar glaze. Never are they frosted.

Coffeecakes are leavened with yeast or baking powder; buns and pastries are always yeast raised. More elaborate recipes may be undertaken in stages, particularly assembled the night before and refrigerated until morning. Many are worth making in double quantity so that the extra can be frozen and reheated later in the month when you have the desire for a memorable breakfast—but no time to prepare one.

Hurry-up Caramel Buns

Easy to make because you use frozen bread dough, these nut-and-cinnamon filled buns are ready even faster if you begin thawing the bread dough in the refrigerator the night before. The baked buns freeze and reheat well.

MAKES 1 DOZEN

> 1 1-pound loaf frozen bread dough
> 1 cup firmly packed light-brown sugar
> ½ cup (1 stick) plus 3 tablespoons butter
>   or margarine, softened
> ¼ cup water
> 1 cup chopped pecans or walnuts
> 2 tablespoons granulated sugar
> 1½ teaspoons ground cinnamon

1. Allow the frozen bread dough to thaw following the package directions.

2. To make the buns' sticky topping, combine the brown sugar, ½ cup butter, and the water in a 1-quart saucepan. Heat to boiling over medium heat; and allow to boil 5 minutes, stirring frequently. Reduce the heat slightly if the sugar syrup boils up too high. Pour the hot syrup into a 10-inch round baking pan. Sprinkle ½ cup nuts evenly over the syrup.

3. On a lightly floured surface, roll the dough out to a 14- by 9-inch rectangle. Spread it with remaining 3 tablespoons butter. In a cup, mix the granulated sugar and cinnamon, and sprinkle over the buttered dough. Sprinkle the dough with the remaining ½ cup nuts.

4. Starting from one long side, roll the dough up, jelly-roll style, pinching to seal the outside edge. Cut the roll into 12 slices and arrange these evenly over the topping in the pan. (Do not worry about small gaps between the rolls.)

5. Cover the buns with a clean cloth. Let them rise in a warm place, away from drafts, until they are double in size, 40 to 60 minutes.

6. Heat the oven to 350°F. Bake the buns 30 minutes, or until they are golden brown. Let them stand 5 minutes, then invert them onto a platter.

Hot Cross Buns

Your kitchen will be filled with the heavenly aroma of cinnamon and nutmeg when you bake Hot Cross Buns. Decorated with a sugar-glaze cross, these buns have long been traditional Easter fare, and a symbol of spring.

MAKES 15 BUNS

> ¾ cup milk
> ¼ cup (½ stick) butter or margarine
> 1 package active dry yeast
> ⅓ cup warm water (105° to 115°F)
> 6 tablespoons granulated sugar
> 2 large eggs
> 4 to 4½ cups all-purpose flour
> 1 teaspoon salt
> 1 teaspoon ground cinnamon
> ½ teaspoon ground nutmeg
> ½ cup dark seedless raisins
> ¼ cup chopped mixed candied fruit

EGG GLAZE:
1 large egg
1 tablespoon water

SUGAR ICING:
1 cup sifted confectioners' sugar
1 tablespoon milk

1. In a 1-quart saucepan, heat the milk until bubbles form around the side of the pan. Remove from the heat. Stir in the butter and cool to warm.

2. In the large bowl of an electric mixer, sprinkle the yeast over the water. Stir in 2 tablespoons sugar. Let stand until foamy, about 10 minutes. With the mixer at low speed, add the remaining 4 tablespoons sugar, the milk mixture, and the eggs until well blended. Beat in 2 cups flour, the salt, cinnamon, and nutmeg until well mixed.

3. At medium speed, beat 2 minutes. Stir in enough of the remaining flour to form a soft dough. Turn the dough out onto a floured surface. Knead it, adding more flour if necessary, until it is smooth and elastic, about 5 minutes. During the last minute or so of kneading, work in the raisins and candied fruit.

4. Lightly oil a large bowl. Place the dough in the bowl, turning to bring the oiled side up. Cover it with a clean cloth and let it rise in a warm place, away from drafts, until it is double in size, about 1 hour.

5. Grease a 13- by 9-inch baking pan. Punch down the dough and shape it into a 15-inch rope. Cut the rope crosswise into 15 pieces. Shape each into a smooth ball, and space evenly in the greased pan. Cover the buns with a clean cloth and let them rise again until they are double in size, about 1 hour.

6. Heat the oven to 375°F. Prepare the Egg Glaze: In a cup, lightly beat the egg with the water.

7. With a sharp, thin-bladed knife, carefully cut a cross, ¼ inch deep, on top of each bun. Brush the tops of the buns well with the glaze. Bake the buns 25 to 30 minutes, or until they are golden brown. Remove them from the pan; cool on a wire rack.

8. Prepare the Sugar Icing: In a small bowl, stir together the confectioners' sugar and milk until smooth. Stir in more milk if the icing is too stiff to drizzle. With the tip of a spoon, drizzle the icing into the cross on each bun.

Glazed Orange-Walnut Sweet Rolls

A sweetened orange butter is the surprise filling for these wonderful sweet rolls. Warm from the oven, they're drizzled with a sugary orange glaze and so, at the table, need no butter, jam, or marmalade.

MAKES 1 DOZEN

1 package active dry yeast
⅓ cup warm water (105° to 115°F)
2 tablespoons sugar
½ cup milk
2 tablespoons butter or margarine
1 teaspoon salt
1 large egg
2¼ cups all-purpose flour

ORANGE FILLING:
3 tablespoons butter, softened
⅓ cup sugar
2 teaspoons grated orange rind
½ cup chopped walnuts

ORANGE GLAZE:
½ cup sifted confectioners' sugar
1 tablespoon orange juice
¼ teaspoon grated orange rind

1. In a large bowl, sprinkle the yeast over the water. Stir in the sugar and set aside until the mixture is foamy, about 10 minutes. In a 1-quart saucepan, heat the milk until bubbles form around the side of the pan. Remove the pan from the heat and stir in the butter and salt. Cool to warm.

2. Stir the milk mixture and the egg into the yeast mixture. Gradually stir in enough flour to make a soft dough. Turn the dough out onto a floured surface and knead lightly until it forms a ball, about 2 minutes.

3. Lightly oil a large bowl. Place the dough in the bowl, turning to bring the oiled side up. Cover it with a clean cloth and let it rise in a warm place, away from drafts, until it is double in size, about 1 hour. Meanwhile, prepare the Orange Filling: In a bowl, combine the butter, sugar, and the orange rind. Grease a 9-inch round baking pan.

4. Turn the dough out onto a lightly floured surface. Roll it to a 12- by 9-inch rectangle. Spread it with the filling and sprinkle with the walnuts. Starting from one long side, roll the dough up, jelly-roll style, pinching to seal the outside edge. Cut the roll into 12 slices and place them in the greased pan.

5. Cover the rolls with a clean cloth and let them rise again until they are double in size, about 30 minutes.

6. Heat the oven to 375°F. Bake the rolls 25 minutes, or until they are nicely browned. Meanwhile, prepare the Orange Glaze: In a bowl, combine the confectioners' sugar, orange juice, and grated orange rind. While the rolls are warm, remove them from the pan in one piece and drizzle them with the orange glaze.

Grilled Sticky Buns

(Photograph, page 61)

Toasting this diner breakfast specialty in a skillet makes sinfully delicious "sticky buns" taste even better. You can bake the sticky buns in advance, and reheat them in the skillet.

MAKES 14 BUNS

> 1 cup milk
> ½ cup granulated sugar
> 1 teaspoon salt
> 1 package active dry yeast
> ½ cup warm water (105° to 115°F)
> 5¼ cups all-purpose flour
> ½ cup (1 stick) butter or margarine, softened
> 1 large egg
> ⅔ cup firmly packed light-brown sugar
> 1½ teaspoons ground cinnamon
> ½ cup light corn syrup
> ½ cup coarsely chopped walnuts or pecans
> ¾ cup dark seedless raisins
> Butter or margarine to grill buns

1. In a 1-quart saucepan, heat the milk until bubbles form around the side of the pan. Remove from the heat. Stir 6 tablespoons granulated sugar and the salt into the milk. Cool to warm. In a small bowl, sprinkle the yeast over the water. Stir and set aside to soften, about 5 minutes.

2. In a large bowl, combine 5 cups flour, the warm milk mixture, the yeast mixture, ¼ cup softened butter, and the egg. Stir with a wooden spoon until a soft dough forms.

3. Sprinkle a board or work surface with the remaining ¼ cup flour. Turn the dough out and knead it until it is smooth and elastic, about 5 minutes.

4. Lightly oil a large bowl. Place the dough in the bowl, turning to bring the oiled side up. Cover it with a clean cloth and let it rise in a warm place, away from drafts, until it is double in size, about 40 minutes.

5. Meanwhile, in a small bowl, combine 3 tablespoons of the remaining softened butter, the brown sugar, ½ teaspoon cinnamon, and the corn syrup. Divide the mixture among fourteen 10-ounce (4½-inch-wide) custard cups. Combine the nuts and ½ cup raisins and sprinkle evenly among the cups. Stir the remaining 1 teaspoon cinnamon into the remaining 2 tablespoons sugar and set aside.

6. Divide the dough in half. On a lightly floured surface, roll out one half to a 16- by 10-inch rectangle. Spread this dough with half the remaining butter; sprinkle with half the cinnamon-sugar mixture and 2 tablespoons raisins. Starting from one short side, roll the dough up jelly-roll style, pinching to seal the outside edge. Cut the roll into 7 slices. Place one slice in each prepared cup. Repeat with the other half of the dough.

7. Cover the buns with a clean cloth and let them rise again until they are double in size, 50 to 60 minutes.

8. Heat the oven to 350°F. Set the custard cups on baking sheets. Bake the buns 25 minutes, or until they are nicely browned. Immediately invert them onto a lightly oiled tray. Cool completely.

9. Just before serving, split the buns in half horizontally. In a large skillet, griddle, or sandwich grill, melt 1 teaspoon butter. Place the buns, 4 halves at a time, cut sides down, in the skillet. Weight the buns with an oiled sandwich press or a heatproof plate. Grill until golden brown. Repeat until all the buns have been grilled, adding butter as necessary. Serve immediately.

Croissants

(Photograph, page 155)

Although time-consuming to produce, nothing can beat the taste of these flaky, buttery crescent-shaped rolls. The French are the acknowledged authority on croissants, and now have a chocolate-filled version called *pain au chocolat.* In our recipe, mashed potato is blended in, varying from the classic recipe, to give the croissants a chewy texture similar to that of professionally-baked croissants. Croissants can be stored in an airtight container and frozen.

MAKES 2 DOZEN

> 1 medium-size (6-ounce) baking potato,
>   peeled and quartered
> ¾ cup milk
> 1¾ cups (3½ sticks) butter
> ½ teaspoon salt
> 2 packages active dry yeast
> 2 tablespoons sugar
> 2 large eggs
> About 4 cups all-purpose flour
>
> EGG GLAZE:
> 1 large egg
> 1 tablespoon water

1. In a 1-quart saucepan, place the potato and enough water to cover. Heat to boiling over high heat. Cover and cook the potato over low heat until it is fork-tender. Drain the potato and reserve ¼ cup cooking water. In a small bowl, mash the potato.

2. In the same saucepan, heat the milk until bubbles form around the side of the pan. Remove from the heat and stir in ¼ cup butter, the mashed potato, and salt. Cool to warm.

3. In a large bowl, place the reserved potato water; cool to warm. Sprinkle the yeast over the water; stir in the sugar, and set aside until foamy, about 10

minutes. Stir in the warm milk mixture and eggs until well combined. Stir in 3 cups flour or enough to make a very soft dough. (The dough should be barely handleable, softer than other bread doughs.)

4. Turn the dough out onto a floured surface. Knead it gently, adding more flour if necessary, just until it forms a soft ball, 1 to 1½ minutes. It should be just barely manageable and will not be elastic. Use a dough scraper to help lift it if necessary.

5. Lightly oil a large bowl. Place the dough in the bowl, turning to bring the oiled side up. Cover it with a clean cloth and let it rise in a warm place, away from drafts, until it is double in size, about 1½ hours.

6. Meanwhile, cut each of the remaining 3 sticks of butter into 8 pieces and place on a sheet of waxed paper. Sprinkle with ⅓ cup flour. With your fingers, quickly work the flour into the butter just until it is blended in but the butter is still firm. If the butter softens, refrigerate it until it is firm again. Shape the butter mixture into a 6-inch square; wrap it in waxed paper and refrigerate it until it has the consistency of vegetable shortening, about 15 minutes.

7. On a well-floured surface, invert the bowl to remove the dough. Do not punch or manipulate the dough or the croissants will be tough. With a floured rolling pin, roll the dough to a 13-inch square. Unwrap the butter and place it diagonally in the center of the dough. Bring the corners of the dough, one at a time, over the butter to meet in the center, overlapping by 1 inch. (The sides of the dough will overlap as well to form an envelope.) Press the edges of the dough to flatten and seal in the butter.

8. With the rolling pin, gently roll the dough to an 18- by 9-inch rectangle. Be sure the edges are even. Do not press too firmly or the butter will be forced out. (In a warm kitchen, if the butter softens too much, transfer the dough to a baking sheet and refrigerate it until it is firm.) Bring one 9-inch end of the dough rectangle over the center third of the dough. Brush off the excess flour and bring the other end over the first to form 3 layers of dough.

9. Roll the dough out again to an 18- by 9-inch rectangle. Fold it crosswise in thirds as before, to form 3 layers. Wrap the dough in plastic wrap and transfer it to a baking sheet. Refrigerate the dough 30 to 45 minutes. Repeat the rolling, folding, and chilling process 2 more times, and refrigerate the dough 1½ to 2 hours the last time.

10. To shape the croissants, cut the dough crosswise in thirds. Work with one piece at a time; wrap and chill the remainder. Roll the dough out on a lightly floured surface to a 13-inch circle. Cut it into 8 wedges. With your fingers, at the wide end of each wedge, pull the points to widen or stretch the base to about 6 inches. Then gently pull the top point of the wedge to lengthen the triangle to about 7 inches. Starting from the base, roll up the triangle. Place the croissant, top-point underneath so that it won't uncurl, on a jelly-roll or pizza pan. Curve and bring the base points toward the center to form a crescent; press the points together to seal. Shape all the croissants, placing them 2 inches apart on baking pans.

11. Cover the croissants loosely with a clean cloth. Let them rise at room temperature, until the dough feels light and spongy, 1 to 1½ hours. On hot days, refrigerate the croissants intermittantly so that the butter is contained.

12. After the croissants have risen, refrigerate them 20 minutes before baking to harden the butter and make them flakier.

13. Heat the oven to 425°F. Prepare the Egg Glaze: In a cup, beat together the egg and water. Brush the glaze over the croissants. Bake them 15 minutes. Remove them from the oven; brush each with glaze again; return to the oven; and bake until they are nicely browned, 1 to 2 minutes. Cool the croissants on wire racks 10 minutes, serve warm.

Chocolate Croissants

Prepare the croissant dough in the basic recipe. On a lightly floured surface, roll one-third of the dough to a 14- by 12-inch rectangle. Cut this into six 7- by 4-inch rectangles. Cut two 3-ounce bars bittersweet or dark chocolate into 6 rectangles, each about 3- by 1½ inches. Brush the edges of the dough with egg glaze. Place the chocolate lengthwise along one short end in the middle and roll to enclose the chocolate completely. Press the seam firmly to seal and place the croissant, seam-side down, on a jelly-roll pan. Cover with a clean cloth; let rise; brush with egg glaze and bake as in the basic recipe.

Blueberry Croissants

Prepare the croissant dough in the basic recipe. Prepare the blueberry filling: In a 1-quart saucepan, combine ¼ cup sugar and 2 tablespoons cornstarch; stir in 1 cup frozen blueberries. Cook over medium-low heat, stirring constantly, until the berries thaw and the mixture boils. Boil 1 minute, stirring, until the mixture is very thick. Remove from the heat and stir in 1 teaspoon grated lemon rind. Cover and refrigerate the filling until it is cold and firm, about 2 hours.

Roll one-third of the dough to a 13-inch circle and cut it into 6 wedges. Pull the top point of each wedge to stretch the triangle to about 7½ inches; pull the base points to stretch slightly. Brush the edges of the triangle with the egg glaze. Place one-sixth of the blueberry filling along the base in the middle of triangle. Roll the triangle once to cover the filling; press the dough around the filling to seal completely. Continue to roll the triangle, pulling the top point as you roll to get more turns in the croissant. Place the croissants on a jelly-roll pan, cover with a clean cloth, and let them rise. Brush them with egg glaze and bake as in the basic recipe.

Danish Pastries

(Photograph, page 155)

Similar to croissants, Danish pastries have less butter—never margarine—and more sugar in their yeast-based dough. And without the potato that's added to our croissants, the pastries are soft, not chewy. You can shape Danish pastries in various ways or fill them with jam or fruit purees. We recommend these simple rounds filled with cream cheese or pureed apricot.

MAKES 14 OR 15 PASTRIES

> 1 cup milk
> 2 packages active dry yeast
> ¼ cup warm water (105° to 115°F)
> ¼ cup sugar
> 1 large egg
> 1 teaspoon salt
> ½ teaspoon ground nutmeg
> About 3½ cups all-purpose flour
> 1 cup (2 sticks) butter
>
> CREAM CHEESE FILLING:
> 1 8-ounce package cream cheese, softened
> ½ cup confectioners' sugar
> 1 large egg yolk
> 1 tablespoon all-purpose flour
> 1 teaspoon grated lemon rind
> OR
> APRICOT FILLING:
> 1 cup dried apricots
> Water
> ⅓ cup sugar
> ¼ teaspoon lemon extract
>
> EGG GLAZE:
> 1 large egg
> 1 tablespoon water

1. In a 1-quart saucepan, heat the milk until bubbles form around the side of the pan. Remove from the heat and cool to warm.

2. In a large bowl, sprinkle the yeast over the water. Stir in half the sugar and set aside until foamy, about 10 minutes. Stir in the remaining 2 tablespoons sugar, the warm milk, egg, salt, and nutmeg. Stir in 2 cups flour and mix the dough until it is smooth. Stir in ¾ to 1 cup flour, to form a soft dough.

3. Turn the dough out onto a floured surface. Knead it gently, adding more flour if necessary, just until it forms a soft ball, 1 to 1½ minutes. It should be barely manageable and will not be elastic. Use a dough scraper to help lift it if necessary.

4. Lightly oil a large bowl. Place the dough in the bowl, turning to bring the oiled side up. Cover it with a clean cloth. Let it rise in a warm place, away from drafts, until it is double in size, 1 to 1½ hours.

5. Meanwhile, cut each stick of butter into 8 pieces and place them on a sheet of waxed paper. Sprinkle the butter with ¼ cup flour. With your fingers, quickly work the flour into the butter just until it is blended. Shape the butter mixture into a 6-inch square. Wrap it in waxed paper and refrigerate it until it has the consistency of vegetable shortening, about 15 minutes.

6. On a floured surface, invert the bowl to remove the dough. Do not punch the dough down or the pastries will be tough. With a floured rolling pin, roll the dough to a 12-inch square. Unwrap the butter and place it diagonally in the center of the dough. Bring the corners of the dough, one at a time, over the butter to the center, overlapping by 1 inch. Press the edges of the dough to flatten and seal in the butter.

7. With the rolling pin, gently roll the dough to an even 18- by 9-inch rectangle. Be sure the edges are even. Do not press too firmly or the butter will be forced out. (In a warm kitchen, if the butter softens too much, transfer the dough to a baking sheet and refrigerate it until it is firm.) Bring one 9-inch end of the dough rectangle over the center third of the dough. Brush off the excess flour and bring the other end over the first to form 3 layers of dough. Roll the dough again to a rectangle; fold, wrap, and refrigerate. Repeat 2 more times.

8. Prepare the Cream Cheese or Apricot Filling, or make half of each.

Cream Cheese Filling: In a small bowl, combine the cream cheese, confectioners' sugar, egg yolk, flour, and lemon rind.

Apricot Filling: In a 1-quart saucepan, place the apricots and water to cover. Heat to boiling over high heat. Cover the pan and cook the apricots over low heat just until they are rehydrated. Remove from the heat and cool to room temperature. Drain well. In a food processor, with the chopping blade, process the apricots until they are smooth. Stir in the sugar and lemon extract until they are well combined. Refrigerate until ready to use.

9. Prepare the Egg Glaze: In a cup, beat together the egg and the water. Cut the dough in half. Work with one half; wrap and chill the other half. On a lightly floured surface, roll the dough to a ¼-inch thickness; with a floured 4-inch round cookie cutter, cut the dough into 7 or 8 circles. With a 2-inch round cookie cutter, cut and remove the center of each circle. Set the dough rings aside. Push the dough scraps together and reroll to ⅛-inch thickness. Cut out 7 or 8 more circles. Place the circles, about 1½

inches apart, on jelly-roll pans. Brush the circles with egg glaze and top with the dough rings. Brush the rings with egg glaze. Spoon 1 tablespoon filling into the center of each pastry. Repeat with the remaining dough.

10. Let the pastries rise, uncovered, at room temperature, until they are light and spongy, about 1 hour. Refrigerate them 15 minutes before baking to harden the butter.

11. Heat the oven to 400°F. Bake the pastries 15 minutes. Remove them from the oven; brush the side of each pastry with egg glaze. Return them to the oven and bake until they are lightly browned, 1 to 2 minutes. Cool them on a wire rack 10 minutes before serving.

Strawberry-Rhubarb Coffeecake

We celebrate the coming of spring with two of the season's best-loved flavors: strawberry and rhubarb. The unmistakable tang of rhubarb harmonizes with the sweetness of strawberries to make a slightly tart yet mildly sweet filling for this coffeecake.

MAKES 12 SERVINGS

> 1½ pounds rhubarb without tops
> 1 16-ounce package frozen, sweetened strawberries
> 2 tablespoons lemon juice
> 2¾ cups sugar
> ⅓ cup cornstarch
> 3¾ cups all-purpose flour
> 1 teaspoon baking powder
> 1 teaspoon baking soda
> ½ teaspoon salt
> 1¼ cups (2½ sticks) butter or margarine
> 1½ cups buttermilk
> 2 large eggs
> 1 teaspoon vanilla extract

1. Trim the ends and any leaves from the rhubarb. Rinse the stalks well and dry thoroughly on paper towels. Cut the rhubarb into 1-inch pieces. (You should have about 3 cups.)

2. In a 3-quart saucepan, combine the rhubarb, strawberries, and lemon juice. Cover and cook over medium heat 5 minutes. In a small bowl, stir together 1 cup sugar and the cornstarch. Gradually stir the sugar mixture into the rhubarb mixture. Heat to boiling; cook, stirring constantly, for 4 minutes. Set aside to cool slightly.

3. Heat the oven to 350°F. Grease a 13- by 9-inch baking pan; set aside.

4. In a large bowl, combine 3 cups flour, 1 cup sugar, baking powder and soda, and salt. Cut 1 cup butter into chunks; add to the flour mixture. With a pastry blender or 2 knives, cut in the butter until the mixture resembles coarse crumbs.

5. In a small bowl, beat together the buttermilk, eggs, and vanilla. Stir the buttermilk mixture into the flour mixture just until combined. Spread half the batter evenly in the greased pan. Spread the rhubarb filling over the batter. Drop the remaining batter by heaping tablespoonfuls over the rhubarb filling.

6. In a 1-quart saucepan over low heat, melt the remaining ¼ cup butter. Stir in the remaining ¾ cup flour and ¾ cup sugar until the mixture resembles coarse crumbs. Sprinkle the crumbs over the top of the batter.

7. Bake the coffeecake 40 to 45 minutes, or until it is golden brown and bubbly. Cool the cake in the pan on a wire rack 10 minutes. Cut it into squares and serve warm.

Best-Ever Cake Doughnuts, page 150   *Old-Fashioned Yeast Doughnuts, page 152*

Finnish Coffee Braid

(Photograph, page 175)

Both the streusel topping and the sugary egg glaze on these stout braided loaves supply that melt-in-the-mouth sweetness so often craved early in the day. One bite and the flavor of cardamom will immediately identify this tender bread's origin as northern Europe, where the spice is used liberally.

MAKES 3 LOAVES

> 2 cups milk
> ½ cup (1 stick) butter or margarine
> 2 packages active dry yeast
> ½ cup warm water (105° to 115°F)
> 1¼ cups sugar
> 4 large eggs, beaten
> 1¼ teaspoons ground cardamom
> 1 teaspoon salt
> 9½ to 10½ cups all-purpose flour
>
> STREUSEL TOPPING:
> 2 tablespoons butter, softened
> 2 tablespoons all-purpose flour
> 2 tablespoons sugar
>
> GLAZE:
> ¼ cup water
> 2 tablespoons sugar
> 1 large egg yolk

1. In a 2-quart saucepan, heat the milk just until bubbles form around the side of the pan. Remove from the heat and stir in the butter. Cool to warm.

2. In a large bowl, preferably of a heavy-duty electric mixer, sprinkle the yeast over the warm water. Stir and set aside to soften, about 5 minutes.

Corn Fritters, recipe page 154

3. Beat the sugar, eggs, cardamom, and salt into the milk mixture and add to the softened yeast. With the mixer on low speed, gradually add 5 cups of flour, beating well after each addition. Let the dough stand 10 minutes.

4. Beat in another 4½ cups flour, until a soft dough forms. With the dough hook of the mixer, knead until the dough is smooth and elastic, adding as much of the remaining flour as necessary to make it manageable, about 7 minutes. Or, turn the dough out onto a floured surface and knead until it is smooth. (Hand kneading will require more flour.)

5. Lightly oil a large bowl. Shape the dough into a ball and place it in the bowl, turning to bring the oiled side up. Cover it with a clean cloth and let it rise in a warm place, away from drafts, until it is double in size, about 60 to 70 minutes.

6. Prepare the Streusel Topping: In a small bowl, with a fork or your fingers, combine the butter, flour, and sugar until crumbly. Set aside.

7. Grease 3 baking sheets. Punch down the dough. Cut and shape it into 9 equal-size balls. Roll each ball into a rope, 14 to 15 inches long. Braid 3 ropes together to form a loaf; place this on a greased sheet. Repeat to make 2 more loaves. Cover the braids with clean cloths and let them rise again until they are double in size, 30 to 45 minutes.

8. Heat the oven to 325°F. Sprinkle topping down the center of the braids. Bake the loaves 25 minutes, or until they are golden brown.

9. Meanwhile, prepare the Glaze: In a cup, beat the water, sugar, and egg yolk until blended. Brush the glaze over the loaves. Bake the loaves 5 minutes longer. Brush again, and bake until the loaves sound hollow when tapped on top. Remove them from the baking sheets and cool on wire racks.

Pennsylvania Dutch Apple-Muffin Cake

(Photograph, page 120)

We like to bake this cake in a charlotte mold, one of those deep round pans with slanting sides, so that it looks like a giant muffin. Still, it will taste just as good baked in a souffle dish or a tube pan—full of the heady autumn flavors of apples, cinnamon, allspice, and cloves.

MAKES ONE 8-INCH CAKE

About 2 tablespoons packaged unseasoned bread crumbs

CRUMB TOPPING:
¼ cup sugar
3 tablespoons all-purpose flour
¼ teaspoon ground cinnamon
2 tablespoons butter

2 cups all-purpose flour
1¼ cups sugar
1 tablespoon baking powder
1¼ teaspoons ground cinnamon
1 teaspoon salt
½ teaspoon baking soda
½ teaspoon ground allspice
¼ teaspoon ground cloves
½ cup (1 stick) butter, melted and cooled
1 cup sour cream
2 large eggs
1 cup finely diced, cored, peeled apple

1. Heat the oven to 350°F. Butter a 2-quart charlotte mold or souffle dish, or a 9-inch tube pan, and sprinkle with the bread crumbs, tapping out the excess. Prepare the Crumb Topping: In a small bowl, combine the sugar, flour, and cinnamon. With a pastry blender or 2 knives, cut in the butter until the mixture resembles coarse crumbs; set aside.

2. In a large bowl, combine the flour, sugar, baking powder, cinnamon, salt, baking soda, allspice, and cloves. In a small bowl, stir the butter, sour cream, and eggs until they are well combined.

3. Stir the butter mixture into the flour mixture just until the batter is smooth and satiny. Stir in the apples. Spread the batter into the prepared mold. Sprinkle with the crumb topping.

4. Bake the cake 1 hour, or until the crumbs are lightly browned and a cake tester comes out clean. (If you are using a tube pan, start testing for doneness after 45 minutes.)

5. Cool the cake in the mold on a wire rack for 20 minutes. Run a metal spatula or knife between cake and the side of the mold to loosen the cake, then gently invert it onto a work surface and remove the pan. Turn it over onto the wire rack and cool completely. Transfer the cake to a serving plate.

Strawberry Pocket Coffeecake

Because this yeast-raised coffeecake requires only one rising before baking, it is manageable for a morning meal. Be sure the strawberry preserves are chilled before spooning them over the dough—cold preserves are less likely to spread during those first minutes in the oven, which means the baked coffeecake will be filled with delicious pockets of warm preserves. If you prefer, you can substitute raspberry preserves or any chunky fruit spread.

MAKES 9 SERVINGS

> 1 package active dry yeast
> 1 cup warm water (105° to 115°F)
> ⅓ cup granulated sugar
> 1 large egg
> ¼ cup (½ stick) butter or margarine, melted and cooled
> 1 teaspoon grated orange rind
> ½ teaspoon salt
> 2½ cups all-purpose flour
> ½ cup cold strawberry preserves
> 1 cup confectioners' sugar
> 2 tablespoons orange juice or milk
> ⅓ cup pecan halves

1. In a large bowl, sprinkle the yeast over the water. Stir in the granulated sugar and set aside until the mixture is foamy, about 10 minutes.

2. Grease a 9-inch-square baking pan; set aside. Stir the egg, melted butter, orange rind, salt, and 1½ cups flour into the yeast mixture until well mixed. Stir in enough of the remaining flour to form a soft dough. Spread or press the dough evenly in the greased pan. Cover the dough loosely with a clean cloth and let it rise in a warm place, away from drafts, until it is double in size, about 1 hour.

3. Heat the oven to 375°F. Drop teaspoons of preserves over the dough; push each drop firmly into the dough with the back of a wooden spoon.

4. Bake the coffeecake 25 to 30 minutes, or until it is golden brown. Cool completely in the pan on a wire rack.

5. In a small bowl, combine the confectioners' sugar and orange juice until smooth. Drizzle half the sugar glaze over the coffeecake; sprinkle with pecans, then drizzle the remaining glaze. To serve, cut the cake into squares.

Cranberry Braid

(Photograph, page 117)

This a fine, handsome sweet bread to bake during the late fall and early winter when cranberries are in season, though you can make it any time with frozen berries. Not only do the fruity flavors of cranberry and orange meld beautifully in the filling, but they are enhanced by the buttery orange-scented dough that's folded, braid-like, over the loaves.

MAKES 2 LOAVES

FILLING:
1 12-ounce package cranberries
1 cup sugar
1 tablespoon cornstarch
⅓ cup orange juice

1⅓ cups water
¾ cup (1½ sticks) butter or margarine, softened
7 to 7½ cups all-purpose flour
2 packages rapid-rising dry yeast
⅔ cup sugar
2 tablespoons finely grated orange rind
1 teaspoon salt
4 large eggs

1.   Prepare the Filling: Rinse and pick over the cranberries. In a 3-quart saucepan, combine the sugar and cornstarch until well mixed. Stir in the orange juice and cranberries. Heat to boiling over medium heat, stirring constantly. Continue to cook and stir until the berries are crushed and the mixture thickens to the consistency of preserves, 10 to 15 minutes. Remove the pan from the heat and cool. Cover and refrigerate until the filling is cold, about 2 hours.

2.   Meanwhile, prepare the Bread: In a 1-quart saucepan, heat the water and butter just until very warm; remove from heat. In the large bowl of an electric mixer, combine 2 cups flour, the yeast, sugar, orange rind, and salt. On low speed, gradually beat the water-butter mixture into the flour mixture until well blended. Beat on medium speed 2 minutes.

3.   Separate 1 egg, reserving the white in a cup, and add the yolk to the flour mixture. Reduce the mixer speed to low; beat in the remaining 3 whole eggs and 2 cups flour and continue beating until it forms a soft dough. With a wooden spoon, stir in enough flour to make a stiff dough. Turn the dough out onto a floured surface.

4.   Lightly oil a large bowl; set aside. Knead the dough, working in more flour if necessary, until it is smooth and elastic, about 5 minutes. Shape the dough into a ball. Place the dough in the bowl, turning to bring the oiled side up. Cover the dough loosely with a clean cloth and let it rise in a warm place, away from drafts, until it is double in size, 1 to 1¼ hours.

5.   Grease 2 baking sheets. Turn the dough out onto a lightly floured surface, and cut it in half. Shape each half into a ball; let these rest 5 minutes. With a floured rolling pin, roll each ball into a 14- by 10-inch rectangle and place them on the greased baking sheets. Lightly brush the top of each with some slightly beaten reserved egg white. Set the remaining white aside.

6.   Spread half the cranberry filling in a 3-inch-wide strip lengthwise down the center of each rectangle to 1 inch from the short edges of the dough. Cut the dough crosswise on each side of the filling into 1-inch-wide strips. Fold the strips alternately across the filling for a braided effect. Cover the braids loosely with clean cloths, and let them rise again until they are almost double in size, about 20 minutes.

7. Heat the oven to 350°F. Brush the braids with the remaining egg white. Bake them 20 minutes; brush them again with egg white and bake 10 minutes longer, or until they sound hollow when tapped on top. Cool the braids on wire racks for 5 minutes, then remove them from the baking sheets and cool completely on the racks.

Peach Streusel Coffeecake

Fresh from the orchard and bursting with the flavor of the sun, peaches are one of summer's treasures. Here they are baked in an almond-scented coffeecake, delicately sweetened with a crumbly streusel topping.

MAKES ONE 9-INCH CAKE

STREUSEL TOPPING:
⅓ cup all-purpose flour
2 tablespoons butter, softened
2 tablespoons light-brown sugar
½ teaspoon ground cinnamon

1¼ cups all-purpose flour
¼ cup granulated sugar
1½ teaspoons baking powder
½ teaspoon salt
¼ cup (½ stick) butter or margarine
¼ cup milk
1 large egg
½ teaspoon almond extract
1 pound fresh peaches, peeled, pitted, and sliced (about 2½ cups)

1. Heat the oven to 400°F. Grease and flour a 9-inch springform pan; set aside. Prepare the Streusel Topping: In a small bowl, with a fork, combine the flour, butter, brown sugar, and cinnamon until crumbly; set aside.

2. In a medium-size bowl, combine the flour, granulated sugar, baking powder, and salt. With a pastry blender or 2 knives, cut in the butter until the mixture resembles coarse crumbs.

3. In a cup, beat together the milk, egg, and almond extract. Stir the milk mixture into the flour mixture until smooth. Spread the batter evenly in the prepared pan. Arrange the peach slices, slightly overlapping, over the batter. Sprinkle the topping over the peaches.

4. Bake the coffeecake 35 to 40 minutes, or until the peaches are tender and a cake tester comes out clean. Cool the cake in the pan on a wire rack for 10 minutes. Run a metal spatula or knife between the cake and the side of pan to loosen; remove the side of pan. Serve the coffeecake warm.

Pecan Coffee Ring

(Photograph, page 118)

Anyone who has ever enjoyed homemade Danish pastry will find store-bought a pale second. The traditional Danish pastry does take time to make but the results are divinely lighter-than-air and sinfully buttery. This recipe demands (and deserves) the freshest, palest butter.

MAKES 1 LARGE OR 2 SMALL RINGS

> 1 cup milk
> 2 packages active dry yeast
> ¼ cup warm water (105° to 115°F)
> ¼ cup sugar
> 2 large eggs
> 1 teaspoon salt
> ½ teaspoon ground nutmeg
> About 3¾ cups all-purpose flour
> 1 cup (2 sticks) butter

PECAN FILLING:
> ⅓ cup all-purpose flour
> 2 tablespoons butter, softened
> 2 tablespoons light-brown sugar
> ½ teaspoon ground cinnamon
> 1 cup chopped pecans
> ½ cup dark seedless raisins

> 1 tablespoon water
> 12 to 16 pecan halves (optional)
> 1 cup sifted confectioners' sugar
> 1 to 2 tablespoons milk

1. In a 1-quart saucepan, heat the milk just until bubbles form around the side of the pan. Remove from the heat. Cool to warm.

2. In a large bowl, sprinkle the yeast over the water. Stir in half the sugar and set aside until it is foamy, about 10 minutes. Stir in the remaining sugar, the warm milk, 1 egg, the salt, and nutmeg. Stir in 2 cups flour and mix until smooth. Stir in 1 cup flour, or just enough to form a very soft dough.

3. Turn the dough out onto a floured surface. Knead it gently, adding more flour if necessary, just until it forms a soft ball, about 1½ minutes. It should be just barely manageable and will not be elastic. Use a dough scraper to help lift it if necessary.

4. Lightly oil a large bowl. Place the dough in the bowl, turning it to bring the oiled side up. Cover it with a clean cloth and let it rise in a warm place, away from drafts, until it is double in size, 1 to 1½ hours.

5. Meanwhile, cut each stick of butter into 8 pieces and place them on a sheet of waxed paper. Sprinkle the butter with ¼ cup flour. With your fingers, quickly work the flour into the butter just until it is blended but still firm. Shape the butter mixture into a 6-inch square. Wrap it in waxed paper and refrigerate it until it has the consistency of vegetable shortening, about 15 minutes.

6. On a floured surface, invert the bowl to remove the dough. Do not punch the dough down or the pastries will be tough. With a floured rolling pin, roll the dough to a 12-inch square. Unwrap the butter and place it diagonally in the center of the dough. Bring the corners of the dough, one at a time, over the butter to the center, overlapping by 1 inch. Press the edges of the dough to flatten and seal in the butter.

7. With the rolling pin, gently roll the dough to an even 18- by 9-inch rectangle. Be sure the edges are even. Do not press too firmly or the butter will be forced out. (In a warm kitchen, if the butter softens too much, transfer the dough to a baking sheet and refrigerate it until it is firm.) Bring one 9-inch end of the dough rectangle over the center third of the dough. Brush off the excess flour and bring the other end over the first to form 3 layers of dough. Roll the dough again to a rectangle; fold, wrap, and refrigerate. Repeat 2 more times.

8. Prepare the Pecan Filling: In a small bowl, combine the flour, butter, brown sugar, and cinnamon with a fork until the mixture is crumbly. Stir in the chopped pecans and raisins; set the filling aside. In a cup, beat the remaining egg with the water to make an egg glaze; set aside.

9. To make 1 large ring, roll the dough out to a 24- by 18-inch rectangle. For 2 small rings, cut the dough in half; keep one half of the dough refrigerated until you are ready to shape it. Roll each half to an 18- by 12-inch rectangle. Brush the rolled dough with some egg glaze; sprinkle with the pecan filling. (Use half the filling in each small ring.) Starting from a long side, roll the dough up, jelly-roll style, pinching to seal the outside edges.

10. Shape the roll in a circle or an oval on a large baking sheet with a rim. (Use a large jelly-roll pan, a pizza pan, or heavy-duty aluminum foil on a flat baking sheet with the edges of the foil turned up to catch any drips.) Pinch the ends together to seal into a ring. With a very sharp knife, make cuts, ¾ inch apart, around the outside edge of ring, cutting to within ½ inch of the center.

11. Twist the cut sections almost flat on the baking sheet so that the filling shows, yet the center is still attached. Overlap the sections slightly, working around the ring. Cover the ring with a clean cloth and let it rise at room temperature, until it is light and spongy, about 35 minutes. After the ring rises, refrigerate it 15 minutes before baking to harden the butter.

12. Heat the oven to 400°F. Carefully brush the ring with the egg glaze; arrange the pecan halves, if desired. Bake the small rings 20 to 25 minutes or the large ring for 30 to 40 minutes. The ring will sound hollow when tapped on top. Remove the coffee ring from the baking sheet and cool it on a wire rack.

13. In a small bowl, combine the confectioners' sugar and enough milk to make a smooth glaze and drizzle it over the pecan ring.

Apple Kuchen

As unpretentious as they are delicious, kuchens are cakes made with a basic batter that is topped with slices of fresh, juicy fruit. Here we've chosen apples, which help keep the cake moist.

MAKES 9 SERVINGS

> 1⅓ cups cake flour
> ¼ cup granulated sugar
> 1½ teaspoons baking powder
> ¼ teaspoon salt
> ¼ cup (½ stick) butter or
>   margarine
> ⅓ cup milk
> 1 large egg
> 2 teaspoons vanilla extract
> 1½ pounds cooking apples, peeled,
>   cored, and thinly sliced
>   (about 3 cups)
> ⅓ cup apple jelly
> 2 tablespoons light-brown sugar
> ¼ teaspoon ground cinnamon

1. Heat the oven to 400°F. Grease and flour a 9-inch-square baking pan and set aside.

2. In a medium-size bowl, combine the flour, granulated sugar, baking powder, and salt. With a pastry blender or 2 knives, cut in 3 tablespoons butter until the mixture resembles coarse crumbs.

3. In a cup or a small bowl, beat together the milk, egg, and vanilla. Stir the milk mixture into the flour mixture just until moistened. Spread the batter evenly in bottom of the prepared pan. Arrange the apple slices in rows, slightly overlapping, over the batter. Cover the pan tightly with aluminum foil.

4. Bake the coffeecake 20 minutes. Remove the foil and bake 10 to 15 minutes longer, until the apples are tender. A cake tester inserted in the center will come out clean. Cool the cake in the pan on a wire rack 10 minutes.

5. Meanwhile, in a 1-quart saucepan, heat the jelly, the remaining 1 tablespoon butter, the brown sugar, and cinnamon to boiling. Brush the syrup over the apples. Cut the kuchen into squares and serve warm.

Walnut Sour Cream Coffeecake

Blending sour cream into the batter gives cake a fine, tender texture. Sandwiched inside this crumb-topped coffeecake is a second layer of sweet crumb mixture for an extra burst of good, nutty flavor.

MAKES ABOUT 12 SERVINGS

> **CRUMB TOPPING:**
> ½ cup chopped walnuts
> 1 teaspoon ground cinnamon
> ½ cup sugar
>
> ½ cup (1 stick) butter or margarine,
>   softened
> ⅔ cup sugar
> 2 cups all-purpose flour
> 1 cup sour cream
> 2 large eggs
> 1 teaspoon baking powder
> 1 teaspoon baking soda
> 1 teaspoon vanilla extract

1.   Prepare the Crumb Topping: In a small bowl, combine the walnuts, cinnamon, and sugar. Set aside.

2.   Heat the oven to 350°F. Grease a 13- by 9-inch baking pan. In a large bowl, with an electric mixer at medium speed, cream the butter and ⅔ cup sugar until light and fluffy. Reduce the speed to low and gradually beat in the flour, sour cream, eggs, baking powder, soda, and vanilla.

3.   With the mixer at medium speed, beat the batter until it is light and fluffy, occasionally scraping the side of the bowl with a rubber spatula. Spread half the batter in the greased pan. Sprinkle with half the crumb topping. Spoon dollops of the remaining batter on top; carefully spread to an even layer. Sprinkle the top with the remaining crumb topping.

4.   Bake the coffeecake 25 to 30 minutes, or until a cake tester comes out clean. Cool the cake completely in the pan on a wire rack. To serve, cut the cake into squares.

Kugelhupf

A pleasantly subtle, delicate, European-style coffee bread, kugelhupf is enriched with sour cream, tenderized with milk, and studded with raisins. It serves as a model for a number of the sweet coffeecakes we set out on the breakfast table, and wouldn't be amiss with any meal.

Makes 1 Loaf

1 cup milk
¼ cup (½ stick) butter or margarine
1 package active dry yeast
½ cup warm water (105° to 115°F)
2 large eggs
¼ cup sour cream
½ teaspoon salt
4½ cups all-purpose flour
½ cup golden raisins
¼ cup wheat germ

1.   In a 1-quart saucepan, heat the milk until bubbles form around the side of the pan. Remove from the heat and stir in the butter. Set aside to cool to room temperature.

2.   In a small bowl, sprinkle the yeast over the water; stir and set aside to soften, about 5 minutes. In a large bowl, beat together the eggs and the sour cream. Add the salt, flour, yeast mixture, and cooled milk mixture. Beat until smooth. Stir in the raisins.

3.   Cover the batter with a clean cloth. Let it rise in a warm place, away from drafts, until it is double in size, about 45 minutes.

4.   Generously grease a 9-inch turk's head mold or tube pan. Sprinkle the inside with wheat germ. Beat down the batter and spoon it into the mold. Cover the batter with a clean cloth and let it rise again until it is double in size, about 45 minutes.

5.   Heat the oven to 350°F. Bake the kugelhupf 55 to 60 minutes, or until it is golden. It will sound hollow when tapped on the top. Cool it in the mold on a wire rack for 10 minutes. Remove the bread from the mold and cool on the rack.

Doughnuts & Fritters

Although they have roots in other lands, doughnuts as we know them are an American invention. Following the lead of the Navajos, who cut a hole in their fried dough to keep it from expanding too much, we poked holes in our fried bread and created tire-shaped doughnuts. Today, doughnut houses dot the landscape. We suggest making your own doughnuts: nothing compares. Hot and fresh, a homemade doughnut just about melts in the mouth. While still warm, it can be glazed or rolled in sugar, or, if you can stand to wait until it is cool, frosted.

Not all doughnuts are round with a hole. Some are solid with a hidden pocket of jelly or cream filling; others are small and round and referred to as "doughnut holes." There are twists, crullers, and puffy beignets, which they eat in New Orleans while watching river boats sidle up the Mississippi.

Doughnut doughs are rich in eggs, butter, and sugar, and most use white flour. The dough should never be overhandled—a soft dough makes a tender doughnut. The best way to fry doughnuts is to fill a heavy, four-quart saucepan or Dutch oven one-third full with vegetable oil. Regulate the temperature with a thermometer and allow it to regain its heat between batches. Do not crowd the pan with doughnuts and turn them only once during frying to eliminate the danger of puncturing them. (If punctured, they will absorb oil.) You will know when they are done by their golden color, but double-check by breaking one open to make sure the middle is cooked through.

Fritters, similar to doughnuts in so many ways, are also deep-fried cakes. The batter for fritters is usually lighter, with less flour, than for doughnuts and often is mixed with vegetables such as corn or fruit such as apples. Country-style food, fritters are as comfortable on a plate with a couple of fried or poached eggs as they are on a dish holding roast chicken. Best of all, they are quick to make and certainly tasty to eat.

Best-Ever
Cake Doughnuts

(Photograph, page 137)

When the morning air turns crisp and cool, make up some of our favorite doughnuts, lightly spiced with cinnamon and nutmeg. Since cake doughnuts are not raised with yeast, preparation time is short. We suggest tossing half the doughnuts (and their "holes") in a mixture of cinnamon and sugar, the other half in plain sugar. Not only does this give everyone a choice, it looks pretty, too.

MAKES 16 DOUGHNUTS AND 16 HOLES

> **3 cups all-purpose flour**
> **1 cup sugar**
> **1 tablespoon baking powder**
> **1 to 1½ teaspoons ground cinnamon**
> **½ teaspoon salt**
> **¼ teaspoon ground nutmeg**
> **1 cup milk**
> **1 large egg**
> **¼ cup (½ stick) butter or margarine,**
> **melted and cooled**
> **1½ quarts vegetable oil, for frying**

1. In a large bowl, combine the flour, ½ cup sugar, baking powder, 1 teaspoon cinnamon, salt, and nutmeg. In a small bowl, combine the milk, egg, and melted butter. Stir the milk mixture into the flour mixture until well combined. Cover and refrigerate the dough at least 1 hour.

2. On a well-floured board, with a floured rolling pin, roll the dough to ½-inch thickness. Using a lightly floured 3-inch doughnut cutter with the center in place, cut out the doughnuts and holes. Pat the scraps together to form 3-inch rounds and cut out more doughnuts.

3. In a 3-quart saucepan, heat 2 inches of oil to 370°F on a deep-fat thermometer. Fry the doughnuts and holes, a few at a time, turning often, until they are golden brown, about 2 to 3 minutes. Drain them on brown paper or paper towels.

4. In a small plastic or paper bag, place the remaining ½ cup sugar. Add ½ teaspoon cinnamon, if desired. Toss the doughnuts and holes in the sugar, a few at a time, until they are coated.

Whole-wheat Doughnuts

To make whole-wheat doughnuts, replace 1 cup all-purpose flour with 1 cup whole-wheat flour.

Oliebollen

Have a large, colorful platter close to the stove when you fry these fruit-filled pockets of sweet dough. Drain them and while they're still hot, roll them in sugar and pile them in a mound on the waiting platter. The early Dutch colonists served these on New Year's Day, but we think they should be enjoyed all year long.

MAKES 2 DOZEN 2½-INCH OLIEBOLLEN

> ¾ **cup milk**
> 2 **tablespoons butter or margarine**
> 1 **package active dry yeast**
> ¼ **cup warm water (105° to 115°F)**
> 6 **tablespoons sugar plus more for coating**
> 2 **medium eggs**
> ½ **teaspoon ground nutmeg**
> ¼ **teaspoon salt**
> 3½ **to 4 cups all-purpose flour**
> 1 **small cooking apple**
> 1 **tablespoon chopped candied citron**
> 1 **tablespoon dark seedless raisins**
> **About 2½ quarts vegetable oil, for frying**

1.   In a 1-quart saucepan, heat the milk until bubbles form around the side of the pan. Remove from the heat. Stir in the butter and cool to warm.

2.   In a large bowl, sprinkle the yeast over the water. Stir in 2 tablespoons sugar and set aside until it is foamy, about 10 minutes. Add the milk mixture, the remaining sugar, the eggs, nutmeg, and salt. With a wooden spoon, gradually beat in 3 cups flour until well combined. Knead the dough in the bowl until the mixture forms a ball.

3.   Sprinkle a board or work surface with ½ cup flour. Turn the dough out onto the board and knead, adding more flour if necessary, until it is smooth and shiny, about 3 minutes.

4.   Lightly oil a large bowl. Place the dough in the bowl, turning to bring the oiled side up. Cover the dough with a clean cloth and let it rise in a warm place, away from drafts, until it is double in size, about 45 minutes.

5.   Meanwhile, core and finely chop the apple. In a small bowl, combine the apple, citron, and raisins.

6.   Lightly oil a baking sheet and set aside. Punch down the dough. Divide it into 24 equal-size pieces. With your hand, flatten each piece and fill its center with some apple mixture. Bring the edges of the dough together to form into a ball, enclosing the filling; pinch the edges tightly to seal. Place the oliebollen on the oiled sheet. Cover them with a clean cloth and let them rise again until they are double in size, about 45 minutes.

7.   Meanwhile, in a 4-quart saucepan, heat 3 inches of oil to 370°F on a deep-fat thermometer. Fry the oliebollen, a few at a time, turning once, until they are golden, about 1½ minutes on each side. Remove them with a slotted spoon and drain on brown paper or paper towels. While they are still warm, roll them in granulated sugar to coat completely. Oliebollen are best served right away.

Old-Fashioned Yeast Doughnuts

(Photograph, page 137)

Doughnuts are sweet pleasures in the morning. Pour your first cup of coffee and leaf through the weekend paper while the dough rises. With the rapid-rising yeast we suggest here, you can have fresh doughnuts with your second cup. This versatile recipe offers you several varieties: jelly-filled doughnuts and plain or sugar-glazed doughnuts or twists.

MAKES 1 TO 1½ DOZEN DOUGHNUTS PLUS HOLES

3¾ to 4 cups all-purpose flour
¼ cup granulated sugar
1 package rapid-rising dry yeast
1 teaspoon salt
1¼ cups very warm water (120° to 130°F)
¼ cup (½ stick) butter or margarine, melted and cooled
1 large egg white, lightly beaten
½ to ⅔ cup seedless red raspberry preserves
About 1½ quarts vegetable oil, for frying
¼ to ½ cup confectioners' sugar

SUGAR GLAZE:
2 cups confectioners' sugar
1 teaspoon vanilla extract
2 to 3 teaspoons water

1.   In the large bowl of an electric mixer, combine 3 cups flour with the sugar, yeast, and salt. Stir in the warm water and butter. With the mixer at low speed, beat until a soft dough forms. With a wooden spoon, stir in enough of the remaining flour to make a stiff dough. Turn the dough onto a floured surface.

2.   Lightly oil a large bowl and set aside. Knead the dough, adding more flour if necessary, until it is smooth and elastic, about 4 minutes. Shape the dough into a ball. Place the dough in the oiled bowl, turning to bring the oiled side up. Cover the dough with a clean cloth and let it rise in a warm place, away from drafts, until it is double in size, 30 to 35 minutes.

3.   Lightly oil 2 baking sheets. Punch down the dough. On a lightly floured board, shape the dough into a ball.

To make filled doughnuts: Roll the dough out to ¼-inch thickness. Remove the center from a 3-inch doughnut cutter and cut the dough into rounds. Re-roll and cut out the scraps. Brush the surface of half of the rounds with egg white; place 2 teaspoons preserves in the center of each. Top with the remaining rounds, pressing firmly around the edge to seal in the preserves. Place the doughnuts on the oiled baking sheets.

To make plain doughnuts: Roll the dough to ½-inch thickness. Using a 3-inch doughnut cutter with the center in place, cut out doughnuts and holes. Reroll and cut out the scraps. Place the doughnuts and holes on the oiled baking sheets.

To make twists: Divide the dough into 18 equal-size pieces for small twists or 12 pieces for large ones. On a floured surface, roll the dough pieces into 6-inch ropes for small twists and 8-inch ropes for large ones. Fold each in half and twist. Place on the oiled baking sheets.

4.   Loosely cover the doughnuts with a clean cloth, and let them rise again until they are double in size, about 45 minutes.

5. Meanwhile, in a 4-quart saucepan, heat 2 inches of oil to 370°F on a deep-fat thermometer. Fry the doughnuts and holes, a few at a time, turning often, until they are golden brown, about 4 minutes. Remove them with a slotted spoon and drain on brown paper or paper towels.

6. While the filled doughnuts are still warm, dust them with confectioners' sugar. If you have made plain doughnuts, prepare their Sugar Glaze: In a small bowl, stir together the confectioners' sugar, vanilla, and enough water to make a smooth mixture. Dip the doughnuts and holes into the glaze. Cool them on a wire rack until the glaze has set.

Funnel Cakes

Common fare in Pennsylvania Dutch farmers' markets, funnel cakes are made by pouring batter through a good-sized funnel spiraled around into hot fat, to produce twisted, thick strands of fried dough. The peculiar-looking cakes are good with sausage and eggs, or by themselves with maple syrup or honey.

MAKES 5 CAKES

> 2 large eggs
> 1 cup milk
> 1¾ cups all-purpose flour
> 1 tablespoon granulated sugar
> 1 teaspoon baking powder
> ¼ teaspoon salt
> About 1 quart vegetable oil, for frying
> ¼ cup confectioners' sugar

1. In a small bowl, with a wire whisk, beat the eggs until frothy. Gradually beat in the milk. Add the flour, granulated sugar, baking powder, and salt. Beat until the mixture is smooth.

2. In a large skillet, heat 1 inch of oil to 375°F on a deep-fat thermometer.

3. Strain the batter into a pitcher. Hold a funnel with a ½-inch opening under the lip of the pitcher and, starting in the center of the skillet, pour the batter through the funnel into the oil, in a spiral, until it is within an inch of the edge of the pan. Fry the funnel cake until it is golden, about 2 minutes. Using two large pancake turners, carefully turn to fry the other side. Remove the funnel cake from the oil. Drain it on brown paper or paper towels.

4. Repeat with the remaining batter. Sprinkle the cakes with confectioners' sugar. Serve warm.

Great American Corn

Corn, in all its varieties, is one of the most thoroughly and creatively used agricultural products in America. By dry-milling, it can be made into grits, meal, and flour. Corn starch, oil, and syrup are obtained by wet-milling and are used in the production of goods as diverse as jellybeans and soap, adhesives and sizing for cloth. Hominy is hulled corn with the germ removed. Popcorn is, well, popped corn. Corn can be distilled into alcohol. And in 1906, Dr. John Harvey Kellogg turned it into cornflakes.

But the tradition of corn on the breakfast table started way before then. American Indians had been cultivating corn—they called it maize—for hundreds of years before introducing it to the early settlers. Today, as in colonial times, inventive American cooks make fritters, as well as corn pones and corn bread, muffins and souffles, hasty pudding, jonnycakes, and succotash.

At farmers' markets and roadside stands, you can find a large selection of corn—mostly of the sweet variety. Also known as sugar corn, this breed wasn't even around back in Pilgrim times; its major development came after 1920. Sweet corn retains greater quantities of sugar than other types of corns, which have longer histories and come under the categories of dent, flint, and popcorn. Dent corn feeds cattle and becomes meal and alcohol. We most commonly see flint corn as the colorful "Indian" corn so often used as decoration. Popcorn can be blue, yellow or white, and in any color it's an emblem of America.

Whether we pop it in the kernel, boil it by the ear, or bake with it as a grain, corn should be relished. It's native, it's delicious, it's downright patriotic.

Corn Fritters
(Photograph, page 138)

Economy is close to the heart of many country cooks, and corn fritters are a most satisfying way to use up cooked ears left over from the night before. You'll need about six medium-size ears to get the two cups of corn called for here.

MAKES 18 SMALL FRITTERS

> 2 large eggs
> 2 cups fresh whole-kernel corn
> 2 tablespoons flour
> 1 tablespoon butter, melted
> 1 teaspoon sugar
> ¼ teaspoon salt
> About ¼ cup vegetable oil, for frying

1. In a medium-size bowl, beat the eggs just to mix them. Add the corn, flour, butter, sugar, and salt. Beat until well blended.

2. In a large skillet, heat the oil over medium heat. Drop spoonfuls of the batter, about 1 heaping tablespoon, into the hot oil. Do not overcrowd the fritters. Adjust the heat to prevent overbrowning, and cook 3 to 4 minutes on each side, until the fritters are light golden brown.

3. Remove the fritters with a slotted spoon and drain on brown paper or paper towels. Serve warm.

(Overleaf)
Gooseberry Jam, recipe page 177
Herbal Apple Jelly, recipe page 170
Old English Lemon Curd, recipe page 171

Croissants, page 132

Fruit Sampler with Yogurt Sauce, page 166

Bagels, page 56

Danish Pastries, page 134

Apple Fritters with Custard Sauce

Mix up the batter for these fritters the night before, or toss it together on the way out the door to attend to morning chores. When you're ready for breakfast, it's quick business to fry up the fritters and serve them with a simple custard sauce. Golden Delicious apples are ideal as they are the least likely to discolor.

MAKES 6 SERVINGS

> 6 Golden Delicious apples, peeled and
>   cored
> ⅔ cup granulated sugar
> ⅓ cup brandy
> ¼ teaspoon ground cinnamon
> 1¾ cups all-purpose flour
> 6 large egg yolks
> 2¼ cups milk
> ⅔ cup beer
> 2 tablespoons butter or margarine, melted
> 1½ teaspoons vanilla extract
> About 1 quart vegetable oil, for frying
> 2 large egg whites, at room temperature
> Confectioners' sugar

1.　Cut the apples into ¼-inch-thick rings. Place them in a large bowl and toss with ⅓ cup granulated sugar, the brandy, and the cinnamon. Refrigerate the apples at least 1 hour, turning occasionally.

2.　To prepare a fritter batter, in a large bowl combine the flour, 2 egg yolks, ¾ cup milk, the beer, and the butter. Stir to blend. Let this mixture stand 1 hour at room temperature.

3.　To prepare a custard sauce, in a 2-quart saucepan combine the remaining 4 egg yolks and the remaining ⅓ cup granulated sugar. Stir in the remaining 1½ cups milk. Cook over medium-low heat, stirring constantly, until the custard coats the back of a metal spoon, about 5 minutes. Stir in the vanilla, and allow to cool to room temperature.

4.　In a large skillet, heat 1 inch of oil to 375°F. In a small bowl, beat the egg whites until they are stiff, then gently fold them into the fritter batter. Drain the liquid from the apples. Dip the apple rings, one at a time, into the batter with a fork or tongs, letting the excess drip back into the bowl. Fry the fritters until they are brown on one side, 1 to 2 minutes, then turn and brown the other side. Drain them on brown paper or paper towels.

5.　Arrange the fritters on a plate, sprinkle with confectioners' sugar, and serve with custard sauce.

Old-Fashioned Peach Preserves, recipe page 172

Beignets

(Photograph, page 176)

Nowhere do folks enjoy a leisurely morning meal more than in New Orleans. On any sunny day in that graceful city, you will find a good number of the citizenry perusing the daily paper while sipping a cup of Café au Lait (page 187) and eating the light, airy doughnuts called *beignets*. Happily, you don't have to be in the French Quarter to appreciate beignets: They taste just fine on a bright, breezy porch or in a sunlit kitchen.

MAKES 15 BEIGNETS

> ½ **cup milk**
> 1 **tablespoon butter**
> 1 **package active dry yeast**
> ¼ **cup sugar**
> ½ **cup warm water (105° to 115°F)**
> 1 **large egg**
> ½ **teaspoon ground nutmeg**
> ⅛ **teaspoon salt**
> 4½ **to 5 cups all-purpose flour**
> **About 1½ quarts vegetable oil, for frying**
> ½ **cup confectioners' sugar**

1. In a 1-quart saucepan, heat the milk until bubbles form around the side of the pan. Remove from the heat; add the butter and cool to warm.

2. In a large bowl, sprinkle the yeast and sugar over the water. Stir to dissolve; set aside until foamy, about 10 minutes.

3. Add the warm milk mixture, egg, nutmeg, and salt to the yeast mixture. Gradually beat in 3 cups flour until the batter is smooth. Add enough remaining flour to make a manageable dough.

4. Turn the dough out onto a floured surface. Knead, adding more flour if necessary, until the dough is smooth and elastic, about 5 minutes.

5. Lightly oil a large bowl. Place the dough in the bowl, turning to bring the oiled side up. Cover loosely with a clean cloth. Let it rise in a warm place, away from drafts, until it is double in size, about 1 hour.

6. Lightly oil a large baking sheet. On a lightly floured surface, roll the dough to a 15- by 10½-inch rectangle, about ¼ inch thick. Cut the dough into 3½- by 3-inch rectangles. Place the beignets on the oiled baking sheet. Cover loosely with a clean cloth, and let them rise again until they are double in size, about 45 minutes.

7. Meanwhile, in a 4-quart saucepan, heat 2 inches of oil to 350°F on a deep-fat thermometer. Fry the beignets, a few at a time and turning often, until they are puffed and golden brown, about 2 minutes. Remove them with a slotted spoon and drain on brown paper or paper towels. Sprinkle them with confectioners' sugar and serve warm.

Breakfast Crullers

These sweet little breakfast treats, made from *choux* pastry batter, are deep-fried, then bathed in a honey glaze. The batter is simple to make—it's the same one that you use for cream puffs and eclairs.

MAKES ABOUT 1½ DOZEN CRULLERS

> 1 cup water
> ¼ cup (½ stick) butter or margarine
> ¼ cup sugar
> ½ teaspoon salt
> 1 cup all-purpose flour
> 3 large eggs
> About 2½ quarts vegetable oil, for frying

> **HONEY GLAZE:**
> 1 cup confectioners' sugar
> ½ cup honey

1. In a 3-quart saucepan over high heat, heat the water, butter, sugar, and salt to boiling. Add the flour all at once. With a wooden spoon, stir until the mixture leaves the side of the pan. Remove from the heat. Cool slightly.

2. Add the eggs, one at a time, beating well after each addition. Refrigerate the batter 15 minutes.

3. Meanwhile, in a 4-quart saucepan, heat 3 inches of oil to 370°F on a deep-fat thermometer. Cut aluminum foil into eighteen 3-inch squares and oil each square.

4. Spoon the batter into a large pastry bag fitted with a large (about ½-inch opening) star or rosette tip. Pipe a 3-inch ring of batter onto each oiled square.

5. Slide the crullers (on the foil) into the hot oil a few at a time. With tongs, carefully remove the foil from the crullers. Fry the crullers, turning once, until they are firm and golden, about 3 minutes. Carefully remove them with tongs and drain on brown paper or paper towels. Cool slightly.

6. As the crullers fry, prepare their Honey Glaze: In a 1-quart saucepan, combine the confectioners' sugar and the honey and stir until smooth. Over low heat, heat just to boiling. Remove from heat. Dip the top half of each cruller in the warm glaze, letting the excess drip back into the pan. Place the crullers, glazed-sides up, on a wire rack over waxed paper until the glaze has set.

Fruit

Imagine breakfast without fruit. No freshly squeezed orange juice, succulent grapefruit, strawberries on the cornflakes, or muffins bursting with blueberries. Unthinkable. Fresh fruit is nature's way of saying good morning.

The brilliant colors of berries, apples and oranges will open those sleepy eyes peering just above the tablecloth; the muted colors of pears, peaches and melons will sooth the morning grouch who rolled grudgingly out of bed. A bite into a luscious, ripe fruit and its juices burst and spill into the mouth. There is no simpler or better way to tempt the palate before a hearty meal. Fruits are treats to both sight and taste that adds the perfect final touch to any lovingly prepared table.

The fruit we expect at breakfast varies with the season and with our moods. Fresh fruit, ripe in its season, is always the best. The fruit has been permitted to develop its matchless flavor and texture as nature intended it to—not under forced, artificial conditions. To benefit most from its goodness, rise a few minutes early on those summer and early fall days when the melons ripen in the fields, the fruit hangs heavy in the orchard, and the berries are plump. Set juicy, golden peaches, crunchy apples, or sun-sweetened raspberries and cantaloupe on the table with freshly baked biscuits or muffins.

In the winter, do not let gray skies or icy winds dissuade you from fresh fruit in the morning. Now is the time for glorious citrus fruit such as grapefruit, navel oranges, and sweet clementines. Pineapples are fresh and good in the market; for a delightful contrast of temperatures and textures, try some chilled pineapple chunks on hot oatmeal. Toss a handful of nutritious dried fruit on your morning cereal or bake it into quick breads and muffins.

Do not overlook tropical fruits such as mangoes, kiwis, and papayas. Their exotic sweetness and juiciness lend unexpected whimsey to dull mornings.

The morning's fruit may be squeezed and in a glass, plain and untampered, or sliced and splashed with milk or heavy cream, but regardless of its incarnation, its place on the breakfast table is indisputed.

Blueberries with Yogurt

Try your morning blueberries topped with fresh plain yogurt or sweetened vanilla yogurt. It's a nutritious, reviving way to start the day.

MAKES 4 SERVINGS

> 3 cups blueberries
> 1 16-ounce container plain or vanilla-
> flavored yogurt

1.   Rinse the blueberries. Dry them thoroughly on paper towels and refrigerate. Chill 4 individual dessert dishes.

2.   To serve, divide the berries into the chilled dishes, and top each with a dollop of yogurt. Spoon the remaining yogurt into a sauce dish.

Frosted Strawberries and Pears

Fast, easy, and beautiful, sugared berries and pears feed the eye as well as the body. Sprinkling the moistened fruit with sugar gives it a frosted appearance that will tempt the most finicky eater.

MAKES 4 SERVINGS

> 1 pint basket strawberries
> 2 ripe Bartlett pears, chilled
> ¼ cup lemon juice
> ¼ cup sugar

1.   Gently rinse the strawberries in a bowl of cold water; drain. Dry them thoroughly on paper towels. Hull the berries.

2.   Peel and core the pears. Cut each pear into slices or bite-size pieces. Dip the pears into a small bowl of lemon juice to prevent discoloration. Dry them thoroughly on paper towels.

3.   Mound the fruit in a glass bowl or compote. Sprinkle with sugar and serve.

Raspberries in Champagne

One of the garden's early pleasures is the harvest of raspberries. The soft, exquisite berries are a luxury to savor. Certainly the first ones to appear deserve their own celebration, and what could be more appropriate than Champagne.

MAKES 6 SERVINGS

> 3½ cups red raspberries
> 1 750-ml. bottle Champagne, chilled

1. Gently rinse the raspberries. Dry them thoroughly on paper towels and refrigerate until they are well chilled. Chill 6 Champagne glasses or tall dessert dishes.

2. To serve, divide the raspberries into the chilled glasses. Pour the Champagne over them and serve immediately.

Berries

Berries should be fully ripened, plump, and uniform in color. Avoid any that are crushed, bruised, or moldy. It is always best to pick berries just before serving, but fresh berries may be stored in the refrigerator for a couple of days. Rinse berries when you are ready to use them, then remove stems, leaves, and for gooseberries, tops and tails.

Grapefruit in Raspberry Sauce

Frozen raspberries are one of the best finds in the supermarket. If you have freezer space at home, stock up on them during the months when fresh are not available. With a food processor or blender, you can make a colorful sauce in minutes—just right to complement juicy sections of pink grapefruit. For an unusual garnish, the peel can be shaped into a "rose." With a small knife, cut the peel from each grapefruit in one continuous spiral. When serving, shape the peel into roses and place one in the center of each plate.

MAKES 4 SERVINGS

> 4 large pink grapefruits, chilled
> 1 10-ounce package frozen raspberries in
>   light syrup, thawed
> Mint sprigs

1. Peel the grapefruits. Cut off the white membrane from the grapefruits and section the grapefruits, catching the natural juices in a bowl. Place the grapefruit sections on a plate and set aside.

2. In a food processor or an electric blender, process the raspberries with ¼ cup grapefruit juice until they are pureed. Strain the raspberries to remove the seeds.

3. To serve, spoon the raspberry sauce onto 4 individual rimmed plates. Arrange the grapefruit sections on the plates and garnish with mint sprigs.

Fruit Sampler with Yogurt Sauce

(Photograph, page 155)

To dress up the breakfast table, serve this simple, honey-sweetened yogurt sauce in scooped-out orange shells. Of course, it will taste just as good spooned into an old crockery bowl and set out alongside the fruit.

MAKES 6 SERVINGS

> 4 large navel oranges
> 1 16-ounce container plain or vanilla-
>   flavored yogurt
> 3 tablespoons honey
> 1 large Red Delicious apple
> 1 ripe Bartlett pear
> 2 kiwi fruit
> ¼ pound seedless red grapes, in small
>   clusters
> Lemon or citrus leaves

1. Finely grate the rind of an orange to get 1 teaspoon grated rind. Set aside. Cut the orange in half horizontally; squeeze to extract its juice and discard the juiced halves. Cut the remaining oranges in half horizontally. With a grapefruit knife, carefully remove the orange sections. Reserve the shells.

2. In a small bowl, combine the yogurt, honey, and orange rind. Cover and refrigerate.

3. Core and cut the apple and pear into slices, and dip them into the orange juice to prevent discoloration. Peel and slice the kiwi fruit.

4. Fill the reserved orange shells with yogurt sauce, and place them on 6 individual plates or a large platter. Arrange the fruit attractively around the orange shells. Garnish with lemon leaves. To serve, spoon the yogurt sauce over the fruit.

Broiled Grapefruit Ambrosia

Towards the end of winter, when you're looking for new ways to serve winter fruit, try a combination of grapefruit and orange, topped with brown sugar and coconut and passed quickly under the broiler.

MAKES 4 SERVINGS

> 2 large grapefruits
> 3 navel oranges
> 1 tablespoon brown sugar
> 1 tablespoon butter or margarine
> ¼ cup shredded coconut

1. Heat the broiler. With a sharp knife, cut the peel and membrane from the grapefruits and oranges. Cut the fruit crosswise into ½-inch-thick slices.

2. In a shallow gratin baking dish or a cast-iron skillet, alternately arrange the grapefruit and orange slices. Sprinkle with brown sugar and dot with butter. Broil the fruit until it is hot and lightly browned, about 5 minutes. Sprinkle with coconut and broil just until the coconut is toasted. Serve immediately.

Warm Fruit Compote

Oven-warm and fragrant, a fruit compote nourishes the soul as well as the body. Ideal for relaxed weekend mornings when the family wanders in for breakfast, our recipe is made with macaroon crumbs and served with rich cream.

MAKES ABOUT 10 SERVINGS

> 1 dozen large, dry almond macaroons
> 1 pound dried apricots
> 1 29-ounce can pear halves
> 1 29-ounce can peach slices
> 1 16-ounce can pitted dark sweet cherries, drained
> 1½ teaspoons grated lemon rind
> 1 tablespoon lemon juice
> ⅓ cup firmly packed light-brown sugar
> ½ cup cream sherry or orange juice
> ½ cup heavy cream or Crème Fraîche (page 84)

1.   In a food processor, with the chopping blade, process the macaroons into crumbs, or crush them with a rolling pin. Butter a 2½-quart shallow baking dish, and sprinkle with half the crumbs to coat. Layer the apricots over the crumbs.

2.   Drain the pear halves and peach slices, reserving half of each syrup. Arrange the pears, peaches, and cherries over the apricots.

3.   Heat the oven to 350°F. In a 2-quart saucepan, combine the reserved syrups, the lemon rind and juice, brown sugar, and the cream sherry. Heat to boiling over high heat.

4.   Pour the hot syrup over the fruit, and sprinkle with the remaining crumbs. Bake 20 to 25 minutes, or until the compote is bubbly. Remove it from the oven and allow it to cool slightly.

5.   Just before serving, whip the cream until soft peaks form. Serve the compote warm, with whipped cream or Crème Fraîche.

Fried Apple Rings

(Photograph, page 21)

Particularly in the South where they are a traditional accompaniment to country ham, sweet, fried apple rings are as likely to turn up on the supper table as the breakfast table. Whatever time of day you choose, here is a simple, tasty way to serve the firm apples of autumn.

MAKES 4 TO 6 SERVINGS

> 4 large, tart, firm cooking apples, cored
> 3 tablespoons butter or margarine
> ¼ cup sugar

1.   Cut the apples into ¼-inch-thick rings. In a large skillet, melt the butter over medium heat. Cook the apple rings in hot butter until they begin to soften and become translucent around the edges. Turn and cook the other side.

2.   When the rings are nearly cooked, sprinkle them with sugar. Cover and cook until the sugar dissolves into a syrup, about 1 minute.

Jams, Jellies, Preserves, Butters & Cheeses

Bread and jam: together, these humble foods epitomize spiritual nourishment. When both are homemade, they are divinely delicious. For country cooks, it is no hard measure to have a pantry lined with colorful jars of summer's bounty; rather, it is a labor of love. Luscious fruits, preserved just as they are poised to peak, bring an unforgettable taste of summer to the morning table, whether you savor the preserves mere days after making them or months later, long after the leaves have fallen from the orchard's trees.

Certainly there is a long, proud tradition of putting up fruits and vegetables for the colder months. In earlier generations, folks gathered together after the harvest to press cider and make apple butter. Vats of apples were cooked over large open fires, which snapped and glowed in the crisp fall air, and neighbors spelled each other stirring the thick butter.

How to Sterilize Jars & Prepare for Processing

Check to be sure your canning jars have no nicks, cracks, or sharp edges that will prevent an airtight seal. Wash the jars, lids, and screw bands or caps and rubber rings in hot soapy water. Rinse. In a 16-quart canner or saucepot with a wire rack, place the jars in enough hot water to cover them. Cover the canner and heat to boiling. Turn off the heat and leave the sterilized jars in the canner until you are ready to fill them.

In a 1-quart saucepan, place the jar lids and screw bands or caps and rubber rings and cover with water. Heat to simmering then remove from heat. Leave the equipment in the water until you are ready to use it.

To fill the jars, remove them from the canner and drain them upside down on a wire rack over pa-

per towels or clean cloths. Meanwhile, reheat the water in the canner to boiling. (The canner should be half-filled with water to process the jars; add more if necessary.) Fill the jars with jam or preserves, leaving a small space at the top; wipe the rims clean. Drain and dry the lids and screw bands or caps and rubber rings. Seal the jars. Heat a separate pot or kettle of water to boiling.

To process jars in a boiling-water bath, place them on the rack in the canner with boiling water. When all the jars are in the canner, add more boiling water so that the level is one inch above the tops of the jars. Do not pour the water directly on the jars. Cover the canner and reheat the water to a boil over high heat. Start counting processing time when the water boils. Reduce the heat to medium-low so that the water boils gently. For a simmering-water bath, start counting processing time when the water just begins to boil. Reduce the heat to low to keep the water simmering.

Remove the jars from the canner and place them on clean cloths or a wire rack. Let them cool to room temperature. After 12 hours, test the lids for proper seal: If the center of the lid can be pressed down, the seal is not adequate. In this case, refrigerate the preserves and eat them within a few days, or reprocess the jars. Label and store jars in a cool, dark, dry place.

Rosy Apple Jelly

Apples, particularly when they're slightly underripe, are high in pectin. To ensure good jelling, select firm, tart apples, about a quarter of them not quite ripe. Since the apples are not peeled (for the pectin), the shiny jelly turns rosy pink.

MAKES ABOUT THREE ½-PINT JARS

> **3 pounds red cooking apples**
> 3 cups water
> 3 cups sugar
> 2 tablespoons lemon juice
> 1 bar paraffin

1.   Remove the stem and blossom ends from the apples, but do not peel or core them. Cut the apples into small chunks.

2.   In a 6-quart saucepot, combine the apples and water. Cover and heat to boiling over high heat. Reduce the heat to low and cook 20 minutes, or until the apples are very tender. Remove from the heat.

3.   Moisten a jelly bag or double thickness of cheese-cloth with water. Spoon the apple mixture into the jelly bag. Tie the bag and let it hang from the knob of a cabinet over a 1-quart glass measuring cup. Or place the bag in a strainer over a bowl. Let drip several hours. If the apple juice does not measure 1 quart, pour a little water into the apples in the bag and allow to drip until the juice has been obtained.

4.   Pour the apple juice into a 4-quart saucepan. Add the sugar and lemon juice. Heat to boiling over high heat, stirring until the sugar dissolves. Continue to boil, stirring occasionally, until the temperature reaches 220°F on a candy thermometer.

5.   Meanwhile, sterilize the jelly jars (page 169). In an empty metal can, melt the paraffin carefully in a saucepan with an inch of boiling water. Remove the jelly from the heat. With a metal spoon, skim off and discard the foam from the surface of the jelly. Ladle the jelly into sterilized jars, leaving ½-inch headspace.

6.   Cover the jelly with ⅛-inch layer of melted paraffin. Be sure the paraffin touches all around each jar to completely seal the jelly. Let stand until the paraffin solidifies and the jelly has cooled. Cover the jars with their lids and label.

Herbal Apple Jelly
(Photograph, page 156)

Prepare the juice for jelly as above, but peel the apples first and add ½ cup chopped herbs to the peeled apples. After skimming off the foam, stir in a few drops of green food coloring.

Ladle the jelly into jars and insert a fresh sprig of herb. Cool and label the jars.

Jellies

If you don't have a jelly bag—which is nothing more exotic than a cotton sack sewn together so that it has no bottom seam— use several thicknesses of cheesecloth to drain the fruit.

Rhubarb Jelly

Springtime is the season for dusky red rhubarb. It's wonderful stewed and baked with strawberries into a pie, and also tasty made into a shimmering jelly. The jelly also makes a first-rate glaze for ham.

MAKES ABOUT THREE ½-PINT JARS

2 pounds rhubarb without tops
3¾ cups sugar
1 3-ounce pouch liquid pectin

1. Trim the ends and any remaining leaves from the rhubarb, and rinse the stalks carefully. Cut the stalks into 1-inch pieces. In a food processor, with the chopping blade, combine the rhubarb and ¼ cup sugar. Process until the rhubarb is very finely chopped.

2. Moisten a jelly bag or several thicknesses of cheesecloth with water. Spoon the rhubarb mixture into the bag. Tie the bag and let it hang from the knob of a cabinet over a 1-quart glass measuring cup, or place it in a strainer over a bowl. Let the rhubarb drip several hours.

3. If the rhubarb juice does not measure 1¾ cups, pour a little water over the rhubarb in the bag. Let this drip until 1¾ cups juice is obtained.

4. Prepare the canning jars, their lids, and screw bands for processing (page 169).

5. In a 4-quart saucepan, combine the rhubarb juice and remaining sugar. Heat to boiling over high heat, stirring constantly, until the sugar dissolves. Stir in the pectin and return the mixture to boiling. Boil, stirring constantly, 1 minute. Remove the jelly from the heat.

6. Skim the foam from the top of the jelly. Ladle the jelly into sterilized jars, leaving ¼-inch headspace. Wipe the jar rims clean. Seal and process the jars in a boiling-water bath for 10 minutes. Cool and label the filled jars.

Old English Lemon Curd

(Photograph, page 156)

Try this rich, buttery spread on toast, warm scones, or muffins. It's easy to make and keeps well for a couple of weeks stored in the refrigerator. If you substitute limes for lemons, the curd will be a touch tangier and equally delicious. Both are good spooned into tart shells for special treats with afternoon tea.

MAKES ABOUT 1¾ CUPS

3 large eggs
½ cup fresh lemon juice
1 tablespoon grated lemon rind
½ cup (1 stick) butter
1 cup sugar

1. In the top of a double boiler, beat the eggs until they are frothy. Stir in the remaining ingredients. Place the top over simmering water, but do not allow the water to touch its bottom.

2. Cook, stirring constantly, until the mixture forms a thick coating on the spoon, 15 to 20 minutes.

3. Spoon the curd into a pint jar. Cool to room temperature. Cover tightly and refrigerate the curd at least 2 hours.

Old-Fashioned Peach Preserves

(Photograph, page 158)

Peaches are a marvelous fruit. Just picked off the tree in mid-summer, their sweet juiciness is sublime. Put up in a sugar syrup and left to sit on a shelf in a cool basement, they develop a taste that's nearly as good as (yet different from) fresh peaches.

MAKES ABOUT EIGHT ½-PINT JARS

> **6 pounds firm, ripe peaches (12 large or**
> **18 medium-size peaches)**
> **5 cups sugar**
> **½ cup lemon juice**
> **1 teaspoon salt**

1. In a 4-quart saucepan, heat 3 inches water to boiling over high heat. With a slotted spoon, add a few peaches to the water; blanch 15 seconds. Remove the peaches to a large bowl of cold water. Drain the peaches and pat them dry with paper towels. Peel, halve, and pit the peaches.

2. In an 8-quart saucepot, combine the sugar, lemon juice, and salt. Cut the peaches into bite-size chunks and add to the sugar mixture. Heat the peach mixture to boiling over high heat, stirring frequently. Reduce heat to low and continue to cook, uncovered, until the fruit is translucent and the syrup is thickened, about 1½ hours. Stir the mixture occasionally. With a metal spoon, skim off and discard the foam as it accumulates on the surface of the preserves.

3. Meanwhile, prepare the canning jars with lids and screw bands for processing (page 169).

4. Ladle the preserves into sterilized jars, leaving ¼-inch headspace. (Keep the preserves simmering while filling jars.) Wipe the jar rims clean. Seal and process the jars in a simmering-water bath for 10 minutes. Cool and label the jars.

Golden Orange Marmalade

It's not sweet, yet it's not exactly tart, either. It's marmalade—that delectable combination of flavors, textures, and colors which seems to have been conceived by someone with a thick slice of toasted, home-baked bread in mind.

MAKES SIX ½-PINT JARS

> **1½ pounds oranges**
> **⅓ cup lemon juice**
> **6 cups water**
> **4 cups sugar**

1. Halve the oranges. Squeeze out the juice and set aside. Remove the pulp and tie it in cheesecloth. Thinly slice the orange peel.

2. In an 8-quart saucepot, combine the peel, the orange and lemon juices, water, and bag of pulp. Heat to boiling over high heat. Reduce the heat and simmer gently about 2 hours, or until the peel is very soft and the liquid is reduced by half.

3. Remove the cheesecloth bag of pulp. Squeeze it well, allowing the juice to run back into the pan. Add the sugar and stir until it dissolves. Heat to boiling over high heat and rapidly boil the mixture until it reaches 220°F on a candy thermometer.

4. Meanwhile, prepare the canning jars with lids and screw bands for processing (page 169).

5. Ladle the marmalade into the sterilized jars, leaving ½-inch headspace. Wipe the jar rims clean. Seal and process the jars in a simmering-water bath for 5 minutes. Cool and label the jars.

Lemony
Pear Preserves

Bartlett pears, in the markets from fall into spring, are mixed here with the refreshing taste of lemon and a touch of cinnamon to make chunky preserves. Spoon some into a small cut-glass bowl the next time your family gathers for a big breakfast—the unexpected flavor of pear preserves will be a pleasant change.

MAKES ABOUT FIVE ½-PINT JARS

> 3 cups water
> 3 cups sugar
> 4 pounds large firm, ripe Bartlett pears
> 1 small lemon
> 1 3-inch stick cinnamon

1. In a 4-quart saucepan, heat the water and 2 cups sugar to boiling over high heat. Remove from the heat. Peel the pears, then core and dice them. As each pear is prepared, add it to the sugar mixture.

2. When all the pears are in the sugar syrup, heat to boiling over high heat. Reduce heat to low; simmer 15 minutes. Thinly slice the lemon and remove its seeds. Add the remaining 1 cup sugar, the lemon slices, and the cinnamon stick to the pear mixture. Continue to cook until the fruit is translucent and the syrup is slightly thickened.

3. With a metal spoon, skim off and discard the foam from the surface of the preserves as it accumulates. Discard the cinnamon stick. Cover the pan and let pears stand overnight in a cool place.

4. Prepare the canning jars with lids and screw bands for processing (page 169). With a slotted spoon, spoon the pears into sterilized jars, leaving ½-inch headspace. Heat the syrup to boiling. Boil the syrup until it is thick and has been reduced by about half. Ladle the syrup over the pears to cover. Wipe the jar rims clean. Seal and process the jars in a boiling-water bath for 15 minutes. Cool and label the jars.

Frozen Strawberry Jam

When the sun barely pokes through the leaden February skies and bright days of summer are no more than a pale memory (or a faint hope), take a jar of this uncooked jam from the freezer. Let it thaw overnight in the refrigerator and you will wake up to the warm taste of July.

MAKES ABOUT FIVE ½-PINT JARS

> 2 pint baskets strawberries, hulled
> 4 cups sugar
> 1 3-ounce pouch liquid pectin
> 2 tablespoons lemon juice

1. Sterilize canning jars with their lids and screw bands (page 169).

2. In a large bowl, use a potato masher or the back of a large spoon to thoroughly crush enough berries to make 2 cups crushed berries. With a rubber spatula, stir the sugar into the crushed berries until mixed. Let stand 10 minutes.

3. In a small bowl, combine the pectin and lemon juice and mix well. Stir the pectin mixture into the berry mixture; continue stirring 3 minutes to blend well. A few sugar crystals will remain.

4. Ladle the jam into the sterilized jars. Cover with lids, then screw bands. Let stand at room temperature for 24 hours, or until the jam sets. Label and freeze the jams to use within 1 year. Or, refrigerate the jams to use within 3 weeks.

Farmhouse Ginger Marmalade

Chunks of gingerroot bathed in thick, sugary syrup make this marmalade a delight on a warm, crumbly muffin or piping hot buttermilk biscuit. Later in the day, try it with roasted meat.

MAKES ABOUT FOUR ½-PINT JARS

> 1½ cups chopped, peeled fresh gingerroot
> 2 cups water
> 2 tablespoons lemon juice
> 3 cups sugar
> 1 3-ounce pouch liquid pectin

1. In a 4-quart saucepan, combine the gingerroot, water, and lemon juice. Heat to boiling over high heat. Reduce the heat to low; cover and cook the ginger until tender, about 30 minutes.

2. Meanwhile, prepare the canning jars with lids and screw bands for processing (page 169).

3. Stir the sugar into the ginger mixture. Return to boiling. Add the pectin and boil rapidly, stirring constantly, for 1 minute. Remove the mixture from the heat.

4. Ladle the marmalade into sterilized jars, leaving ½-inch headspace. Wipe the jar rims clean. Seal and process in a boiling-water bath for 10 minutes. Cool and label the jars.

Finnish Coffee Braid, page 139

JAMS, JELLIES, PRESERVES, BUTTERS & CHEESES 175

Café au Lait, Louisiana Style, page 187   *Beignets, page 160*

Gooseberry Jam

(Photograph, page 156)

Gooseberries, like their cousins the currants, make excellent jam and jelly. Cook gooseberries when they're green (unripe) or pink to red (ripe). They are at their best for preserving when half are ripe enough to give the jam a nice red color.

MAKES ABOUT SIX ½-PINT JARS

> 2 quarts gooseberries
> 1½ cups white grape juice
> ½ to ¾ cup orange juice
> 5 cups sugar
> 1 1¾-ounce package powdered pectin

1. Remove the stems and leaves from the gooseberries, then rinse them thoroughly. In a 5-quart Dutch oven, heat the berries and grape juice to boiling over high heat. Reduce the heat to low and simmer the fruit gently for 20 minutes. Remove the pan from the heat and cool the berries slightly.

2. Meanwhile, prepare the canning jars with lids and screw bands for processing (page 169).

3. Spoon the cooked berries, a cup at a time, into a sieve or strainer placed over a 1-quart glass measuring cup or a large bowl. With the back of a wooden spoon, press the berries to extract their pulp. Add enough orange juice to the gooseberry pulp to measure 1 quart.

4. In a 4-quart saucepan, heat the gooseberry pulp to a rolling boil over high heat, stirring constantly. Stir the sugar into the berry pulp. Return to boiling, then add the pectin. Boil rapidly, stirring constantly, 1 minute. Remove the jam from the heat.

5. With a metal spoon, skim off and discard any foam from the surface of the jam. Ladle the jam into sterilized jars, leaving ½-inch headspace. Wipe the jar rims clean. Seal and process the jars in a boiling-water bath for 10 minutes. Cool and label the jars.

Fresh Strawberry Butter

With a melon-ball scoop, create tiny balls of this pretty pink butter, textured with bright red bits of strawberry. Mound the butter balls on a small serving plate and set it on the table to give the morning meal a festive look. Strawberry butter, as you can well imagine, is wonderful on griddle cakes, nut breads, and plain toast.

MAKES ABOUT 1⅓ CUPS

> 1 cup (2 sticks) unsalted butter, at room temperature
> ½ cup finely chopped fresh strawberries
> 2 tablespoons confectioners' sugar

In a small bowl, with an electric mixer at medium speed, beat all the ingredients until well combined. There will be pieces of fruit remaining in the butter. Pack the butter into a small crock or serving bowl. Cover tightly and refrigerate. Allow the butter to stand at room temperature for 30 minutes before serving.

Herb Butter

Just stir herbs fresh from the kitchen garden into softened butter to make a tasty, pretty green spread for bagels or toast. Let the butter chill for 24 hours to give the herbs time to infuse it with their exquisite flavors. And do experiment with other herbs.

MAKES 1 CUP

> 1 cup (2 sticks) butter, softened
> 2 tablespoons chopped fresh chives or tops of green onions
> 2 tablespoons snipped fresh dill or ½ teaspoon dried dillweed
> 2 tablespoons chopped fresh parsley leaves

In a small bowl, mix all the ingredients until well combined. Pack the butter into a small crock or serving dish. Cover tightly and refrigerate. Allow the butter to stand at room temperature for 30 minutes before serving.

Orange Butter

Pat some orange butter on hot waffles or pancakes or spread a little on a bran muffin. Finely grated orange rind adds a pleasant hint of citrus to the sweetened butter, but to avoid even a trace of bitterness, be sure to grate only the bright orange rind, not the underlying white pith. Orange butter is best made ahead of time, so its flavor can develop.

MAKES 1 CUP

> 1 cup (2 sticks) unsalted butter, at room temperature
> 2 tablespoons confectioners' sugar
> 2 tablespoons finely grated orange rind

In a small bowl, mix all the ingredients until well combined. Pack the butter into a small crock or serving bowl. Cover tightly and refrigerate. Allow the butter to stand at room temperature for 30 minutes before serving.

Cranberry Butter

A knob of fruit butter is a gracenote to any ordinary breakfast. Fall is the time for cranberries, which we've sweetened and added here to fresh butter.

MAKES ABOUT ½ CUP

> 1 tablespoon drained Cranberries in Syrup (page 85)
> ½ cup (1 stick) butter, softened

In a bowl, beat the cranberries into the butter. Spoon the cranberry butter into a serving dish or individual crocks, then cover and refrigerate until completely chilled.

Apple Butter

(Photograph, page 59)

In earlier times, making apple butter was a laborious process. We have devised a recipe where the apples are cooked in the oven for several hours and require stirring only occasionally. But the fragrant scent of the slowly cooking apples will keep you in the kitchen.

MAKES ABOUT FOUR 1-PINT JARS

> 6 pounds cooking apples
> 1 cup apple cider or water
> 2½ cups granulated sugar
> ½ cup firmly packed brown sugar
> 2 teaspoons ground cinnamon
> 1 teaspoon ground nutmeg
> 2 tablespoons lemon juice

1. Peel, core, and slice the apples into eighths. Place them in an 8-quart saucepot. Add the cider or water and cover tightly. Heat to boiling over medium heat, stirring to break up the apples and prevent sticking. Cover and cook 15 minutes.

2. Uncover the pot and continue cooking until the apples are soft, 3 to 5 minutes.

3. Heat the oven to 350°F. Stir the remaining ingredients into the cooked apples. Spoon the apples into a large, deep baking dish or casserole. Bake 3 to 4 hours, stirring occasionally, until the mixture is thick and dark. At the right consistency, a spoonful should have almost no liquid surrounding it. Meanwhile, prepare the canning jars, their lids, and screw bands for processing (page 169).

4. Ladle the apple butter into the sterilized jars, leaving ¼-inch headspace. Wipe the jar rims clean. Seal and process the jars in a boiling-water bath for 5 minutes. Cool and label the jars.

Honey Almond Butter

Nut butters deserve a special place on the breakfast table. Their richness enhances a bland piece of toast. This butter, made with sweet, toasted almonds and golden honey, is really very simple to prepare in a food processor.

MAKES ABOUT 1¼ CUPS

> 1½ cups blanched whole almonds
> 3 tablespoons vegetable oil
> ½ cup honey

1. Heat the oven to 350°F. On an aluminum foil-lined jelly-roll pan, spread the almonds. Bake 10 minutes, until the nuts are toasted, stirring or shaking the pan occasionally. Cool the almonds completely.

2. In a food processor, with the chopping blade, process the almonds until they are finely ground. Add the oil, a small amount at a time, processing and stopping occasionally to scrape the side of the container with a rubber spatula.

3. Add the honey to the almond mixture and continue to process until a peanut-butter-like consistency forms.

4. Spoon the almond butter into a jar or crock. Cover tightly and store in the refrigerator. Allow almond butter to stand at room temperature 30 minutes before serving.

Rich Homemade Cream Cheese

As you might expect, fresh homemade cream cheese has a flavor superior to the mass produced version. What you may not expect is that it is fairly simple to make, and requires no special equipment.

MAKES ABOUT 3½ CUPS OR 1½ TO 2 POUNDS

> 6 cups (1½ quarts) milk
> 4 cups (1 quart) heavy cream
> 1 cup plain yogurt
> 1 rennet tablet
> ¼ cup cold water

1. In a nonaluminum heavy, 4-quart saucepan, combine the milk, cream, and yogurt. Heat the mixture over low heat, stirring occasionally, until it reaches 100°F, 30 to 45 minutes.

2. In a cup, dissolve the rennet tablet in the water. Add this to the warmed milk mixture. Stir just until the mixture becomes creamy and thick, 30 to 60 seconds. Remove the pan from the heat; cover and let stand until the curd separates from the whey, 1 to 1½ hours. (The temperature should drop no lower than 85°F. If it does, reheat the cheese slowly.)

3. Cut the curd into 1-inch cubes. Let these stand undisturbed 15 minutes. Line a large strainer or colander with 4 layers of cheesecloth. Place this over a large bowl to catch the whey. Pour the curds into the lined strainer, refrigerate, and allow them to drain overnight. Discard the whey.

4. The next day, remove the cheese from cloth. It can be used immediately by itself, in a cheese spread, or for baking. Or, add ½ to 1 teaspoon salt; wrap in plastic wrap and refrigerate up to 1 week.

Danish Orange Cheese Spread

On lazy weekend mornings when you're in the mood for pancakes or freshly baked muffins slathered with a creamy spread, try this extra-rich recipe. A few tablespoons of softened butter enrich fresh cream cheese, confectioners' sugar sweetens it, and orange liqueur gives it a mellow flavor. We call this one delicious indulgence.

MAKES ABOUT 1¼ CUPS

> 1 cup Rich Homemade Cream Cheese or
>   1 8-ounce package cream cheese,
>   softened
> 2 tablespoons butter, softened
> 2 tablespoons confectioners' sugar
> 1 tablespoon orange-flavored liqueur
> Grated rind of 1 orange

1. Place the cream cheese in a medium-size bowl. In a small bowl, blend the butter, sugar, liqueur, and orange rind until smooth.

2. Gently fold the butter mixture into the cream cheese. (Do not stir too vigorously or the spread will thin down.) Pack the spread into a crock. Cover tightly and refrigerate. Allow the spread to stand at room temperature for 30 minutes before serving.

Acorn Squash Cheese Spread

If you have one or two family members who shun sweet spreads, make up a batch of our savory cream cheese. Acorn squash, chopped dates, and chutney give the spread texture.

MAKES ABOUT 2¼ CUPS

> 1 medium-size acorn squash
> 1 cup Rich Homemade Cream Cheese
>   (page 180) or 1 8-ounce package cream
>   cheese, softened
> ¼ cup (½ stick) butter, at room temperature
> ¼ cup chopped pitted dates
> 2 tablespoons drained, chopped chutney

1.   At the pointed end of the squash, cut off a 1-inch-thick slice to expose the seeds. Scoop the seeds from the cavity and discard.

2.   In a 2-quart saucepan, heat 1 inch water to boiling over high heat. Place the squash, cut-side up, with its top slice back in place, in the boiling water. Reduce the heat to low; cover and simmer just until the squash is fork-tender, about 15 minutes.

3.   With a slotted pancake turner, lift the squash to drain and cool completely on paper towels.

4.   In a small bowl, with an electric mixer at low speed, beat the cream cheese and butter until fluffy. Scoop out the flesh of the cooled squash and add to the cream-cheese mixture.

5.   Beat cheese mixture until well mixed. With a rubber spatula, fold in the dates and chutney. Pack the spread into a crock. Cover tightly and refrigerate. Allow the spread to stand at room temperature for 30 minutes before serving.

Lancaster County Breakfast Cheese

(Photograph, page 59)

The Pennsylvania Dutch make a soft cheese called *schmierkase,* using sour milk and rich dairy cream. We have simplified the recipe by combining cottage cheese with heavy cream to make a smooth, creamy spread. If you choose to use milk rather than cream in the recipe, the spread will be lighter and thinner.

MAKES ABOUT 2 CUPS

> 1 16-ounce container creamed cottage
>   cheese
> 2 to 4 tablespoons heavy cream or milk

In a food processor or blender, combine the cottage cheese and 2 tablespoons cream. Process until smooth. The mixture should have the consistency of sour cream; if necessary, add more cream. Spoon the cheese into a pint jar. Cover tightly and refrigerate. The cheese may be refrigerated for 1 week.

Beverages

The hot beverage most readily associated with breakfast is coffee; the cold beverage is orange juice. Rich, astringent coffee wakes us up. Cool, sweet orange juice tastes of sunshine and new beginnings. Tea, hot, mulled cider, hot chocolate, grapefruit juice, even homemade lemonade and a creamy milkshake also have special places on the morning table.

Coffee varies in flavor and strength. A number of factors contribute to these variations, including the kind of bean, where it was grown, and how it was roasted and processed. Most coffee lovers find that buying whole beans and grinding them just before brewing insures the best cup. Some purists buy unroasted, light-colored beans to roast at home. So many varieties of coffee bean— both caffeinated and decaffeinated—are available today at specialty stores and coffee shops that it makes good sense to experiment with them, mixing two or three to discover your favorite blendings. Generally, although not always, darker beans produce the most intense flavor. Italian espresso beans are nearly black, while the beans for American-style coffee are medium-brown. The best decaffeinated coffee is water-processed, a technique which does not rely on chemicals to remove the caffeine.

Methods for brewing coffee vary, too. Most connoisseurs prefer the drip method, where boiling water is poured over freshly ground coffee. Still, percolated coffee tastes good to a lot of people, too. The choice is yours. The best coffee starts with cold water; bottled water, without chemicals or mineral deposits, makes a noticeable difference.

Cold water, set to boil on the stove, is also the best way to begin a cup of tea. As with coffee, tea varies according to where it is grown and how it is processed. The tea we drink most in the United States is fermented, or black, tea. Unfermented tea becomes Chinese green tea, and partially fermented tea is called oolong or brown tea.

To make a good pot of tea, begin by warming up a ceramic or porcelain pot with a rinse of hot water. The minute the water boils (do not let it bubble away on the stove any longer than you must), it should be poured into the pot over loose tea leaves, measured so that there is a teaspoonful for each cup and one for the pot. The tea then should steep for three to five minutes.

As welcoming as a hot mug of coffee or nice cup of tea is to many at the morning meal, not everyone likes a jolt of caffeine. Hot chocolate, smooth, creamy, and mildly rich, is a nice alternative on snowy days. Mulled, spiced cider is another good choice, particularly on those first sharp, cold days of autumn when everyone needs to be warmed down to their toes.

Juice is best when freshly squeezed, and with a good citrus juicer, it really takes very little time or effort. These cold drinks taste especially good when the menu includes hot pancakes or waffles, eggs, bacon . . . just about anything!

Beverages in the morning are an integral part of the meal. Hot or cold, they round it out—and afford us the chance to pour another cup of coffee or glass of juice and linger just a little longer at the table.

Summer Sun Tea

Glistening like a jewel, a big glass jar of sun tea captures all the downhome flavor of summer in the country. The recipe couldn't be simpler—just tea bags steeped in cold water—and you can try different herb teas to find your family's favorite. Make sun tea the day before and keep it refrigerated.

MAKES 6 SERVINGS

>   4 tea bags
>   1½ quarts cold water

In a glass jar, combine the tea and cold water. Cover and steep in the sun several hours. Serve it in tall glasses with ice and lemon, if desired.

Buttermilk Banana Cooler

Fresh buttermilk marries wonderfully with the sweetness of bananas and honey to produce a cool, filling drink. Add an egg and this could serve as breakfast all by itself.

MAKES 2 SERVINGS

>   2 cups buttermilk
>   2 large ripe bananas, cut into
>   chunks
>   ¼ cup honey

In an electric blender, combine the buttermilk, bananas, and honey. Blend until smooth and frothy.

Old-Fashioned Lemonade

Once you taste homemade lemonade, you will have a hard time buying it frozen or pre-mixed again.

MAKES 4 SERVINGS

>   6 or 7 lemons
>   ½ to ¾ cup sugar
>   1 quart cold water

1.   Thinly slice 2 lemons. In a 1½-quart pitcher, combine the lemon slices and ½ cup sugar. Press the fruit with a potato masher or wooden spoon to release its juice.

2.   Cut and squeeze the remaining lemons to extract ⅔ cup lemon juice. Pour this into the pitcher along with the cold water and stir. Taste and add more sugar, if desired.

Raspberry Shrub

For a festive breakfast, garnish each glass of fruit juice with a skewer of fruits: a rolled half-slice of orange, a kiwi wedge, and a fresh raspberry.

MAKES 4 SERVINGS

>   1 pint raspberry sherbet
>   2 cups orange juice
>   1 tablespoon lemon juice

In an electric blender, combine the sherbet, orange juice, and lemon juice. Blend until smooth.

Strawberry Milkshakes

For breakfast? Why not? On a weekend morning when the kids are slow to come to the breakfast table, whip them up some milkshakes. Sweet, smooth, and filling, the milkshakes are, after all, made from fruit and milk.

MAKES 2 SERVINGS

> 1 10-ounce package frozen strawberries, partially thawed
> 1¾ cups milk
> 1 cup strawberry ice cream

In an electric blender, combine the strawberries, milk, and ice cream. Blend until smooth and frothy.

Chocolate Malted

Try an icy, refreshing malted for breakfast on a sultry summer morning.

MAKES 1 SERVING

> 2 tablespoons chocolate malted-milk drink powder
> 1 cup milk
> ½ cup chocolate ice cream

In an electric blender, combine the malted-milk drink powder, milk, and ice cream. Blend until the malted is smooth and frothy.

Mimosa

Glide into Sunday with this graceful pair. Do make fresh orange juice, if you can; after all, fine Champagne deserves it.

MAKES 12 SERVINGS

> 3 cups fresh orange juice, chilled
> 1 750-ml. bottle Champagne or sparkling wine, chilled

Pour equal amounts of orange juice and Champagne into tulip-shaped wine glasses and serve.

Bellini

This exotic Champagne drink was created at Harry's Bar in Venice, Italy. There the juice of white peaches is sweetened, then blended with sparkling wine. Since it's difficult to find this fruit, we've substituted a white-peach liqueur called Pêcher Mignon.

MAKES 4 SERVINGS

> ½ cup Pêcher Mignon, chilled
> 1 split (8 ounces) Champagne or sparkling wine, chilled

Pour the peach liqueur into tulip-shaped wine glasses. Add the Champagne and serve immediately.

Tranquillity Spiced Tea

A good spiced tea, enlivened with fruit juices and cinnamon, is a welcome treat on those dark winter mornings when you wonder if spring will ever make an appearance. Relax, sip your cup of steaming, aromatic tea. Spring will come. It always does.

MAKES 8 SERVINGS

>   5 cups cold water
>   ½ cup sugar
>   1 3-inch stick cinnamon
>   1 tablespoon whole cloves
>   2 juice oranges
>   2 lemons
>   3 tea bags
>   ½ cup unsweetened pineapple juice

1. In a 1-quart saucepan, heat 2 cups water, the sugar, cinnamon, and cloves to boiling over high heat, stirring to dissolve the sugar. Reduce the heat to low and simmer 10 minutes.

2. Meanwhile, cut the oranges and lemons in half and squeeze to extract their juice.

3. In a 3-quart saucepan, heat the remaining 3 cups water to boiling over high heat. Remove from the heat and add the tea bags. Cover and brew 5 minutes. Remove the tea bags and strain the spice mixture into the tea. Add the orange, lemon, and pineapple juices. Return to the heat and simmer until the tea is piping hot.

Tea

To make a great cup of tea, always start with cold water. Bring it to a full boil before pouring it over a tea bag or leaves in a preheated pot or cup. Let the tea steep to the desired strength. Never boil tea.

Hot Mulled Cranberry Cider

For those who welcome a respite from coffee and tea, our soothing, gently spiced cranberry cider will be a happy substitution.

MAKES 8 SERVINGS

>   1 32-ounce bottle cranberry juice
>   cocktail
>   1 32-ounce bottle apple juice
>   6 cinnamon-apple herbal tea bags
>   8 long sticks cinnamon

1. In a 3-quart saucepan, heat the cranberry juice and apple juice to boiling over high heat. Remove from the heat and add the tea bags. Cover and brew 5 minutes.

2. Remove the tea bags and ladle the cider into mugs. Place a cinnamon stick in each mug.

Hot Chocolate

Creamy and comforting—real hot chocolate is everyday winter fare in the country kitchen.

MAKES 4 SERVINGS

>   1 quart milk
>   4 1-ounce squares semisweet chocolate,
>   chopped
>   4 teaspoons sugar
>   1 teaspoon vanilla extract
>   1 cup sweetened whipped cream
>   3 tablespoons shaved milk chocolate

1.   In a 2-quart saucepan, heat the milk just until bubbles form around the side of the pan. Remove from the heat. Beat the chocolate into the milk with a wire whisk or hand beater.

2.   When the chocolate is melted, add the sugar and vanilla and stir to dissolve the sugar. Pour the hot chocolate into cups and top with whipped cream and chocolate shavings.

Shaker Spiced Apple Cider

Here is our favorite fall breakfast recipe: Take one brisk, windy morning; add one basket of freshly baked muffins; serve with mugs of hot, spicy cider.

MAKES 6 SERVINGS

> 1½ quarts apple cider
> 2 tablespoons light-brown sugar
> 1 3-inch stick cinnamon
> ½ teaspoon whole allspice
> ½ teaspoon plus 6 whole cloves
> 6 lemon slices

1.   In a 3-quart saucepan, combine the apple cider, brown sugar, cinnamon stick, allspice, and ½ teaspoon cloves. Heat to boiling over medium heat. Reduce the heat to low, and simmer 15 minutes, stirring several times to dissolve the sugar.

2.   Insert one whole clove into the center of each lemon slice and place the slices in mugs. Ladle the hot cider over the lemon slices and serve.

Café au Lait, Louisiana Style

(Photograph, page 176)

Stirring hot, rich milk into morning coffee is a decidedly luxurious way to start the day. The French have long followed the practice, and French settlers in New Orleans maintained it. In the late 18th century, owing to a coffee shortage, these innovative drinkers began adding a little chicory to the coffee—and have continued to drink it this way ever since.

MAKES 4 SERVINGS

> 3 cups boiling water
> ½ cup ground Louisiana coffee with chicory
> 2 cups milk
> ⅓ cup heavy cream

1.   Using a drip coffeemaker, brew strong coffee, pouring the water over the ground coffee. Keep the coffee hot.

2.   In a 1-quart saucepan, heat the milk and cream over medium heat just until bubbles form around the side of the pan. (Do not boil.) Pour the milk and cream into a warmed serving pot or pitcher.

3.   Pour about 1 inch of freshly brewed coffee into each of 4 coffee cups. Then simultaneously pour more coffee and warm milk and cream into each cup.

Coffee

For coffee with a French-country flavor, add a dash of cinnamon before brewing. This will give the coffee a mild aroma and a spicy flavor.

Mint Julep

The elegant, easygoing style of the South is captured in this classic cocktail. Traditionally Mint Juleps are served in their own special silver cups, but 12-ounce highball glasses are acceptable. One change, however, cannot be made: Fresh mint is essential here.

MAKES 4 SERVINGS

> 4 teaspoons sugar
> 4 teaspoons water
> 16 sprigs mint
> 3 cups shaved or finely crushed ice
> 1½ cups bourbon

1.   Into each chilled, silver mint-julep cup or 12-ounce highball glass, place 1 teaspoon sugar, 1 teaspoon water, and 3 sprigs mint. With a wooden spoon, crush the mint leaves and stir to dissolve the sugar.

2.   Discard the mint. Fill each cup three-fourths full with ice. Add the bourbon and stir gently. Garnish each with 1 of the remaining mint sprigs.

Citrus

Squeeze citrus fruits as close as possible to the time of use. Nothing beats the flavor of fresh-squeezed citrus juice, as a drink or an ingredient.

Tequila Sunrise

It's February . . . it's snowing . . . and it's Sunday morning. Perhaps a Tequila Sunrise would be in order. A specialty of the sunny-Caribbean, this cocktail is sublime.

MAKES 2 SERVINGS

> 1 cup fresh orange juice, chilled
> 3 ounces tequila
> 2 tablespoons fresh lime juice
> 2 teaspoons grenadine, or to taste
> 2 lime slices

Pour equal amounts of orange juice, tequila, and lime juice into 8-ounce stem glasses. Stir these to blend. Slowly pour 1 teaspoon of grenadine into each glass and allow it to settle. Garnish the rim of each glass with a lime slice.

Bloody Mary

Here is the traditional, all-American breakfast and brunch drink. Garnish each glass with a small, leafy celery stalk.

MAKES 2 SERVINGS

> 1 cup tomato juice, chilled
> 3 ounces vodka or tequila
> 2 teaspoons fresh lemon or lime juice
> 1 teaspoon Worcestershire sauce, or
>   to taste
> 2 dashes hot red-pepper sauce

Pour the tomato juice, vodka, lemon juice, Worcestershire, and hot-red pepper sauce into tall glasses. Stir to mix well and add ice cubes, if desired.

Index

Picture Credits

	Page
Jessie Walker	1
Keith Scott Morton	2
Keith Scott Morton	4
André Gillardin	21
Dale Wing	22
Richard Jeffery	23, Inset
Charles Gold	24
Steve Lovi	41
Victor Scocozza	42
Dennis M. Gottlieb	59
Jessie Walker	60
Jerry Simpson	61, Inset
Dale Wing	62
Dale Wing	79
Graham Kirk	80
André Gillardin	97
Lucy Wing	98
Jessie Walker	99, Inset
Joshua Greene	100
Linda Burgess	100, Inset
Charles Gold	117
Keith Scott Morton	118
Dale Wing	118, Inset
Charles Gold	120
Dennis M. Gottlieb	137
Jessie Walker	138
Richard Jeffery	138, Inset
Dale Wing	155
Jan Baldwin	156
Richard Jeffery	157, Inset
Richard Jeffery	158
Glenn Wolff	164
John Uher	175
Richard Jeffery	176
Beth Krommes	Woodcuts 12, 14 16, 28, 48, 66, 86, 104, 112, 126, 148, 162, 168, 182

All others are courtesy of Dover
Publicatons, Inc., New York, NY